So You Want To Be A School Administrator?

The Sure Fire Way to Land That Principal or Superintendent Job

Charles A. Hall

Writers Club Press

San Jose New York Lincoln Shanghai

Published by Writers Club Press
an imprint of iUniverse.com, Inc.

For information address:
iUniverse.com, Inc.
620 North 48th Street
Suite 201
Lincoln, NE 68504-3467
www.iuniverse.com

ISBN: 0-595-09149-0

Printed in the United States of America

Contents

Foreword

When I sought my first job as a teacher and coach, I like many of my colleagues, learned about résumés from college professors, and stumbled through the job application process. Fortunately, I found a job, and as I moved about, became more adept at landing a teaching job.

I did some reading about job application when I applied for my first school administration job. All of the books I found provided information about writing cover letters, résumés, and participating in job interviews. It was not until I met the author that I discovered that the entire procedure for landing a school administrator job was entirely different than the books that I had read.

This book illustrates beautifully, the science of preparing for, and landing a school administration job. It is packed full of information about what employers are looking for, and how to develop a winning résumé. The author covers the smallest details, from the type of clothes to wear to analyzing the interviewers to "connect" with them. His collection of most common questions asked is extremely helpful in preparing for interviews.

I have used the author's techniques while landing two administrative positions. This is the type of book that school leaders need in order to be competitive in the job market.

Gary Martin, Principal
Steilacoom High School
Steilacoom, Washington

Preface

As a high school principal and superintendent of schools, for two decades, I reviewed countless letters of introduction, résumés, and conducted innumerable interviews. I was surprised by the poor preparation that people put into applications for employment. I saw many qualified individuals miss out on the job because of poor grammar in letters of application and poor interview techniques. I have interviewed scores of school board members and administrators to find out what turned them off to some candidates, and on to others.

I scoured the Internet and bookstores to find a book that might help administrator candidates prepare themselves for the task of finding that dream job. I was unable to find very many books. Instead I found a myriad of books explaining how to land a job in about every other industry.

Unfortunately, the hiring process in the academic world is entirely different than in the other sectors. Too many candidates have read the books about how to land a job in management and been disappointed that the process was not the same when trying to get that job as a building principal. So throw away all those general books on job search! I have put together a step-by-step handbook for teachers that want to be administrators and for administrators that want to climb the ladder to the central office or the superintendency.

Acknowledgements

Thanks to the many public school administrators that inspired me to write this book. Without their encouragement I would not have embarked on a research project that would not only lead to a career as an author, but as a consultant. I would like to thank the countless authorities and sources consulted in the publication of this handbook. Scores of people contributed their information and ideas.

Specifically, a special thanks to: Dr. Doyle Winter, Executive Director, Washington Association of School Administrators' and Dr. Gay Selby, Search Consultant, Washington State School Directors' Association, for their assistance as reviewers; Clarke J. Stone, of The Stone Press who edited the manuscript; Annie Copeland, creative design; Larry Robinson, electronic assistance; and Katherine Hall for administrative assistance.

This book is dedicated to the men and women that devoted themselves to educating the children of this nation. And to the tens of thousands that took up the leadership mantle and made a difference in the lives of not only the children, but also the public school employees.

Finally, to the people that cared enough about our kids to run for, or applied for the office of school board members. Without all these committed individuals, we would not have an educational system that prepares *all* of our children for the future.

Introduction

This is a step-by-step handbook to land the job in school administration that you covet. You have worked very hard to get through college and land the job that you now have. If you want to take the next step—whether it is to get into school administration or move up in school administration, take the approach that it is a hard job and you must put a great deal of effort into it.

If you want to "run with the big dogs," you have to learn how to "separate yourself from the pack." Almost everyone that applies for the same job as you is well-qualified. Unfortunately the best-qualified person does not always get the job. It is your responsibility to convince them that you are better qualified, and will fit in with the other employees and community.

Chapter 1

You Have To Plan Ahead

Background

Have you ever tried to play a game where everybody knew the rules but you?

That's what happens when most certificated employees apply for jobs in school administration. They read a "how to land a job" book and think they know the procedure. They are surprised and disappointed when they find out the entire system is different when schools hire administrators.

You can fill a small library with "how to" books on finding employment—but very few *mention* employment as a public school administrator. If you follow the plan of action outlined in this handbook, you will not only prevent embarrassment but also beat out your colleagues for that coveted administrator's job.

The long-range plan

You should have a long-range plan and a short-range plan. The long-range plan includes your ambitions in school administration. If you are a teacher now and want to be a superintendent, your long-range plan will be longer. The person who has been a superintendent in a smaller district for several years and wants to be a superintendent in a large school district will have a shorter long-range plan.

The long-range plan runs the gamut from enhancing a résumé for the entry-level administrator job to the steps to become a superintendent of a large school district. Some people want to stop at a level some where between, such as a principal of an elementary school or superintendent of a medium size school district.

The long-range plan should be written in pencil because it will change. Sometimes circumstances beyond your control occur that effects your decisions. For example, you may live in a small town now and plan to eventually be a superintendent in a large district in ten to fifteen years. A serious illness in your family occurs, making it impossible to move to a larger community. Your long-range plan may then stop at being superintendent of a small school district.

The short-range plan

The short-range plan is the one you use when you have applied for an administrative position. That should be a written plan and follow the format of this workbook. There are a few rules to follow in seeking employment:

Get ready

Now is the time to position yourself for your next job. Go to work to land it now. Get ready for the day you apply.

Let's take a look at how to prepare for a job you are not currently interested in landing. Do your best at the job that you have. Whenever a supervisor or community member tells you that you have done a good job, tell them politely that you appreciate their comments. However, you would appreciate it if they put it in writing so that you can make it a part of your placement file. There is no harm in asking. Most people will be happy to oblige you.

Establish a placement file

If you don't already have a placement file established at your college or university, do so right away. Keep it updated annually and work to improve the contents.

Get certified

Sign up for classes to become certified in your first or next step in administration. You are showing your current employer that you are ambitious. At the same time, when you do want to seek that new job, you already have the required certification. They had a saying in Vietnam, "stuff happens." Something unexpected could happen to your supervisor, making her unable to continue with her job. With the certification, you have told your supervisors that you are interested in moving up and you are prepared.

Make it easy for them

Each year, review all the letters of recommendation in your placement file and update as necessary. Pay particular attention to letters written by your supervisors. For example, your immediate supervisor may leave her job unexpectedly and not have time to update your placement file. It will be difficult to explain to a search committee that you have a year or two in your work history not covered by a letter of recommendation.

Help your supervisor and yourself by providing a list of topics that you would like covered in your letter of recommendation. I have had situations where supervisors have told me that they would love to write a letter, but don't have the time. I wrote the letters—and they signed them.

In that situation you enjoy the best of both worlds—you not only help your supervisor accomplish a chore, but you have a letter written *by a dynamite writer, about a super employee!*

Always remember to provide your writer a stamped, self–addressed envelope addressed to your placement file custodian. Make it as easy as you can for the person to get your letter in your file.

Awards enhance a good résumé. In most cases, you don't have any control over honors you receive, but there are many awards in the field of education that let you nominate yourself. When you put these nominations on your résumé, you don't have to specify "self-nominated."

Write articles for your professional magazines and get your master's thesis published. A résumé can be enriched with published articles. Employers like to see you can express yourself in writing.

Join at least one service organization, such as Kiwanis or Lions Club. Employers like to see administrators make a commitment to the community, to give time and energy to it. Once in the club, seek leadership positions. Employers are impressed when you seek out leadership in everything you do.

Become a member of the Principal's Association or Administrator's Association, even if you are not a school administrator.

Volunteer to be a member of a school or district planning committee. You are not only showing a commitment to the organization, but it gives you more opportunities to network.

Get acquainted with school board members. Attend as many school board meetings as possible. You learn about news in the district as well as how board meetings are conducted. If a board member has a business, frequent it whenever possible. Take the opportunity to thank board members for their volunteerism.

Get a mentor

Find an administrator that is willing to mentor you. Don't be satisfied with just any mentor. Check to be sure that he or she not only has the time and energy, but also has contacts in the state that can benefit your goals.

Attend conferences with your mentor so that you can spend leisure time as well as get advice about which work sessions to attend. The mentor can introduce you to other administrators. At the conferences ask her to introduce you to other administrators and school board members.

When pursuing advanced degrees and administrator credentials, look for mentors from the instructional staff. University professors usually have contacts throughout the country. Many of them are former administrators and school board members.

Search consultants, commonly known as "headhunters," often attend the conferences of the profession they are trying to hire from. The best way to get their attention is to give them the respect that they deserve. They are the best salespeople in the world. They are the only ones that sell products that talk back.

Introduce yourself to them and buy them a cup of coffee. You can learn from them, as well as let them know that you will be in the job market.

Ask search consultants

- Which are the best districts to work in?
- What employment vacancies are projected for the future?
- What are the qualifications employers are looking for?
- What can you do to prepare for one or more of the vacancies?

Tell them something about your background. Two rules in dealing with search consultants: Tell the truth. Reduce your discussions to the bare essentials to the extent possible.

Meet as many building and central office administrators as possible. Search consultants sometimes ask superintendents or retired superintendents to screen applicants' files for them. Name recognition can move your employment packet to the top.

Volunteer for committees and leadership positions. You are helping your boss do their job, learning more about your profession, and adding to your résumé. This is especially important for the educator that is looking for a first job in administration.

Attend as much leadership training sessions and professional conferences as possible. You will learn more about your profession, what is "on the cutting edge," and have more opportunities to network.

Stay put

Never quit your job until you have another position. Once you become unemployed, you have separated yourself from the pack but in a negative way. It raises a red flag to potential employers. They may believe you were fired, even if you had quit your job voluntarily.

You are personally affected by the situation, and it shows during interviews. You are dealing from a position of weakness instead of strength. Employers want someone that others want. They want people with winning track records.

Be professional

Be professional in everything you do—twenty–four hours a day. Professionalism does not necessarily mean being strict and formal. It means, "having professional spirit or methods." It means that you are humane, and have a good sense of humor. You know what you are doing, but are willing to take advice. You are a good listener and are a "team player." Do this and you will be successful at your job.

A professional:

- Has integrity. It means that your words and deeds match up.
- Is loyal. You are loyal not only to your boss, but also to the organization. Is enthusiastic. Sometimes a project is boring and difficult.·
- Is enthusiasm encourages others to help get the job done.
- Recognizes that people are the most valuable asset. More people lose their jobs because they cannot get along with other employees or customers, then for any other reason.

Get committed

Looking for a job is like having a job: once you make the decision to look for a job, it takes total commitment. Getting the job is not any easier than doing a job. Keep reminding yourself that most of the other applicants for the job are just as able as you—or better qualified. Tell yourself occasionally that the best-qualified person does not always get the job.

The procedure for employment in school administration is not like the practice for other jobs. I will refer to the jobs outside of school administration, under the heading of "general employment," or "general jobs." Throw away all those slick, colorful books full of advice about cover letters, résumés, and interview techniques. Better yet, give them to those that are competing with you for the position.

Public school employment vacancies are not usually advertised in the newspaper. They are advertised in professional publications, in professional organizations, in colleges and universities, and in many cases through direct mailings to individuals. The American Association of School Administrators, National Association of Secondary School Principals, and the National Association of Elementary School Principals have job postings at their web sites.

Most administrative professional organizations publish vacancy announcements. They usually start in January of each year and run through the end of August. Some are published year round. Get a subscription to these announcements and start reading them.

In some cases search consultants make personal contacts with administrators to encourage them to apply for a vacancy. Sometimes they are looking for minority candidates or individuals with special training.

In most cases a brochure is printed by the searching school district. It describes the job and the professional and personal qualities sought in the candidates. It states the salary range; the name, location, and size of the school and district; the closing date for applicants; whom to direct your questions to; and the address to which to mail your application. The brochure will explain what paperwork is necessary and the timetable for hiring.

The vacancy announcement sometimes provides only the vacant position, the school and school district, and contact information for the person handling inquiries. In that case, call the contact person and ask for a brochure. If none is available, ask questions to get the answers usually found in the brochure.

Hiring procedures are different in almost every school district. For example, some districts hiring an administrator have an intermediate interview by a personnel director, then an interview by a committee of staff and community members, followed by a final interview by the superintendent. Be sure you find out what method each district uses.

Districts hiring a superintendent are different, too. Some districts hire a search consultant who screens application packets, interviews candidates, and provides the school board a list of three to five finalists to interview. Some districts invite citizens to the interview. You must be prepared for whatever they throw at you, so it is critical to know the precise procedure followed by each district. For more information about the importance of precisely following a hiring process, see Chapter Six.

Read the brochure carefully. Be sure your application packet follows the brochure to the letter, and submit your packet on time. Only in rare instances will a school district accept an application after the final date listed in the brochure or advertisement. If a confidential placement file is to be sent directly to the school district or search consultant, wait a few days and call the contact person to be sure it arrived. I *didn't* do that once, and I was not interviewed because my placement file never arrived.

Before you apply for the job

Update your placement file, even if you haven't had a job change. Call your college or university and have them send a copy of your paperwork and a list of the letters of recommendation in your file. Go to your boss, tell her that you are seeking employment as an administrator, and ask for a current letter of recommendation. Ask her to keep your job search confidential.

If you are a teacher, seeking your first job in administration, simply say that you are going to try to "spread your wings." If you are currently an administrator, just explain to her that you are not unhappy with your current job. You just want to see what is available out there. You may have some other specific reason, such as a need to relocate your family or a natural progression up the career ladder. Keep your job search confidential. If you don't get the job, you don't want to go through a period where people in your district think you would rather be somewhere else.

It is important to have your supervisor's support because she will be the first person a potential employer will contact. One day a colleague called to tell me one of my principals had applied for a vacancy in his school district, and he wanted to ask about his job performance. After a long pause, he said, "You didn't know he applied, did you?" When I told him no, my colleague told me that he was no longer interested in the applicant.

Find at least three co-workers or people who work for you that are not only supportive, but can be trusted not to tell others that you are seeking a job elsewhere. These people will be used as character references on your job application form. Employers will want to know how you interact with peers and subordinates. They will be looking for information on your leadership style.

If you are a principal, seeking a job in the central office or as superintendent of schools, get as a character reference, a member of the teacher's association, a classified employee—secretary or custodian—and a vice principal or another building principal. It is always helpful to have references from people in a variety of positions.

If you are a superintendent seeking a job as superintendent in another district, get the president of the school board, a principal, the head of the teacher's association, and the head of the classified union. They will probably be contacted if you are a finalist, so it is best to have them on your side *before* they are contacted.

Prepare the people you choose as character references thoroughly. Tell them why you are applying for employment elsewhere. Tell them what you perceive as your strengths in dealing with them. Tell them your management style and some accomplishments you would like them to mention. Type the relevant information on a 5"x8" card for them so they will have the answers when they get a telephone call from someone checking references. They will appreciate your help.

I should note here that if you have had a difficult relationship with union heads, now is the time to use them as references. They may want you to take your "unreasonable attitude" elsewhere and, while they may not lie to help you, they will certainly not complain about you. The same would be true of a school board member with which you have had difficulties.

Unfortunately I have experienced the other side of the coin. A supervisor damned me with faint praise. When I found out why I did not get an interview, I confronted him, and he explained he didn't want to lose a good administrator.

Some districts would like to talk with community members. Put together a list that you can give to the interview committee. But be sure and prep the character references the same as you did for the school employees and board members.

Which jobs do I apply for?

One approach is the "rifle." Another course is the "shotgun." The rifle method is to decide which jobs you are really interested in, and apply only to those. The shotgun approach is to apply for all of the vacancies for which you are qualified.

You could take a "rifle" approach and only apply for the jobs that really interest you or you could take a "shotgun approach and apply for every job for which you are qualified; but I recommend what I call the "selective shotgun" approach: eliminate all jobs you are not qualified for, then eliminate all jobs you are certain you do not want, and apply for whatever jobs remain.

Remember that a job interview is not only for the hiring school district but for the applicant as well. For every rejection, you should learn something that will help you eventually get a position. If at any time during the hiring process you decide that it's not a good fit, withdraw your name from consideration and analyze your experience.

If you realize that the job does not fit your needs, withdraw immediately, especially if you discover you cannot give the district what they want. You may be hired, but you may not be happy with the job. If you can't give them what they want, whatever that is, you are destined for failure, and it will not be long before you are back in the job market—but dealing from a position of weakness, perhaps unemployment (the weakest position of all).

A word of caution: if you withdraw from too many job applications, you can get a reputation for being too selective. Search consultants will start to shy away from you.

Important Points:

1. Get ready
   - Establish and maintain a placement file at your college or university.
   - Work on Administrator's credentials.
   - Look for opportunities to get letters of recommendation.
   - Look for opportunities for awards.
   - Write articles for publication in professional magazines.
   - Be a joiner—service organizations, professional organizations, civic groups, committees, etc.
   - Find a mentor and work at "networking."
   - Get to know search consultants.
   - Attend as many leadership workshops as possible.
2. Don't quit your job unless you have found another.

3. Be professional at all times.
    • Once you decide to take part in the job search, be totally committed.
    • Review the instructions in this book and follow them closely.
    • Get on mailing lists for position vacancies.
    • Learn their hiring procedures.
    • Read and study employment brochures for every position.
    • Update your placement file.
    • Find and prepare character references.
    • Get your supervisor's support.
    • Keep your job search confidential.
    • Use a "selective-shotgun" approach to applying for employment.
    • Don't forget that a job interview is for you as well as the potential employer. If at any time you don't think the fit is right, it's OK to withdraw.

Chapter Two

The First Impression

The cover letter

Now let's sit down and start your cover letter. The cover letter is the first thing seen by a potential employer, so it is your first impression. Remember that you don't get a second chance to make a good first impression.

More is definitely better! "General job" applicants are told to keep the letter to *one* page. Cover letters for administrators don't have such limitations. That doesn't mean that you should ramble on ad nauseam. I'm not saying that a good cover letter will guarantee you a job, but it will get someone to read the rest of your application packet.

Naturally, the teacher with only five years' experience who is applying for her first vice principal's job will have a shorter cover letter than someone who has had twenty years as a teacher, vice principal, and principal. If the letter runs two or three pages and the information you provide is relevant, so be it.

Don't be afraid to provide some of the same information that is in your application form and résumé. Sometimes busy consultants, administrators, school board members, and committee members scan the résumé and read the cover letter carefully—or visa versa.

Tailor every cover letter specifically for the job you are seeking. Use a computer to draft your document. Many copy shops such as Kinko's have computers that can print résumés from your disk. They will let you take your disk to their computer, make your adjustments, then print as many copies as you need.

Make no mistake—every new hire is made on the candidate's ability to satisfy the following expectations of the school district:

1. Ability: Includes such duties as curriculum leadership, improved test scores, safety, and finance.
2. Willingness to work long hours. Strong work ethic.
3. Problem solving skills.
4. Positive response to constructive criticism.
5. Strong support of community. Is a team member.

Your letter must reflect all of those concerns. Concise clear sentences with active verbs help to convey that message. Remember the acronym, **KISS**—Keep It Simple, Stupid. Not all readers of your letter are as well educated as you. Even if they are, the jargon may be different from state-to-state.

Use a good, high quality, white bond paper. Stay away from the colored paper that so many people think attracts the eye of the reader. *It just makes it harder to read!*

This is your first big test in the job search. It is the beginning of the execution of the game plan. The paper should have a letterhead, but not a logo. Most computers have the capability to produce attractive letterheads. Use a block letter format with one blank line between paragraphs.

Use a simple writing style. All school administrators are required to write clearly and accurately. Remember people with all different educational backgrounds could be reading your letter.

Double-space the complimentary closing and triple-space the signature line. And don't forget to sign the letter. I can't tell you how many unsigned cover letters I have seen.

It is important that the letter is clean, with no spelling or grammatical errors. Mistakes show potential employers that you are careless. Run it through the various checks on your computer and have someone else proof it for you.

The brochure

The school district usually prints a very colorful brochure announcing the vacancy. Sometimes the brochure can be transmitted electronically. Remember they are trying to attract as many good applicants as possible. They are trying to sell you on their schools and district. The average brochure usually contains the following information:

1. The name and location of the school or district and a picture of it.
2. A short description of the school, district, and community.
3. The contract provisions. The salary is usually "competitive."
4. The selection process and a timeline showing the dates written applications are to be complete and submitted; dates for paperwork; dates for screening and interview(s); and the date the selected administrator is to report for duty.
5. The application process, stating the name and address of the person who gets the paperwork and the name of the person handling questions. The paperwork normally includes a cover letter (or letter of application), application form, résumé, a placement file, and a list of character references. Sometimes placement files are not required. Instead letters of recommendations, a more extensive list of references from previous positions, and college transcripts are submitted.
6. A very important part of the brochure is a list of challenges and qualifications. They give you some insight into what is expected. A sample brochure follows this page.

Sample Brochure

SUPERINTENDENT OF SCHOOLS
Cripple Creek, WA, School District

Challenges for Superintendent of Schools

* Prepare for and manage the district's growth and changing student demographics to meet the educational needs of all students.
* Maintain and improve effective lines of communication with staff and community that develop trust, confidence, high morale, and continued pride in the "Cripple Creek" schools.
* Develop a financial plan to make the wisest use of available funds to maintain and improve the excellent educational programs in the district.

Qualifications of Superintendent of Schools

* It usually lists the education and experience that they desire in applicants. More importantly the average brochure contains statements such as this:
* In addition to knowledge, skills and experience in all areas of a superintendent's responsibilities, the Board expects the superintendent to:

* Be definitely interested in the total well being of every child.
* Be dedicated to excellence in education. Improve student learning.
* Be a visionary leader who keeps current with educational issues and research and is sensitive to the individual and collective educational needs of all students.
* Be a creative team leader who encourages and promotes staff and community input and involvement in recommendations given to the board. Be visible and actively involved in a fast growing community.
* Be appreciative and sensitive to students and community members of diverse ethnic and racial backgrounds.
* Be able to effectively manage the district's finances and curriculum development.
* Be able to motivate and work effectively with all staff in a collaborative manner.
* Be a team builder, able to reflect genuine appreciation and respect for others.
* Be honest, energetic, caring, and open in dealing with staff and community

No employment brochure:

Some school districts choose not to print brochures. If none is available, call the school district's Human Resources office. Ask the director the following questions to give you some insight into the requirements of the job.

Ask Personnel Director

- How many students are in the school or district?
- How many assistants will you have?
- Why did the person who had the job leave?
- What does she think the administration and school board expects the person they hire to do?
- What sort of personal qualities does she think the new person should have?
- Does she think they are looking for someone to continue the status quo or to make changes?
- What is the salary and benefits package?

The more you know about the school and district, the better chance you have to make a good impression in your cover letter. If they are using a search consultant, telephone her and ask the same questions. Also ask the search consultant the following questions about the process the district is using to arrive at the final hire.

Ask Search Consultant

- Who will screen the records?
- How many interviews will take place?
- Who will be members of the interview committee?
- When will the finalists be announced?

Take notes

You will use some of this data in your cover letter, so collecting as much information as possible can place you ahead of the other applicants.

Be friendly and respectful

You should be respectful, but do not be afraid of asking too many questions. If you are friendly and respectful, they are usually flattered that you value their opinion. If they are the first employees in the district that you meet, they will form the first impression of you. The human resources secretary can have an influence on who is hired, especially in small school districts.

My human resource secretaries usually gave me their opinion of the applicants whether I asked for it or not. Further, they have access to the screening and interview committees. If they gave me their opinion, why wouldn't they do the same for the committee members?

Composing the cover letter or letter of application

Generate interest with the letter. Have a strong first paragraph and keep following through with effective comments, primarily about who you are. The final statement should be you could help make an excellent district into an exceptional district. Say it strong, simple, and powerful—use personal experiences whenever possible. You have to convince the reader you are smart, enthusiastic, and a problem solver. You can help prove it by the contents of your cover letter.

Address *all* of the *qualifications* and *challenges* in your cover letter. You must show your potential employers you are the most qualified applicant and have the skills they are seeking. Some search consultants prefer the *qualifications and challenges* be addressed in the body of the letter, while others prefer that they are separate from the letter.

A sample cover letter that responds to the *challenges* and *qualifications* is on the following pages. Note the letter is addressed to the person who is to receive the packet of paperwork.

Sample Cover Letter

Joseph Cool

19 Elm Street NW   Georgewood, NJ 13579

(515) 555–9753

January 29, 2000

Mr. Mark Time
President, Board of Directors
Cripple Creek School District #123
Cripple Creek, WA 98321

Dear Mr. Time:

I am enthusiastically applying for the position of superintendent of Cripple Creek School District. I have studied the announcement brochure for the superintendent opening, and I am convinced that my qualifications match the challenges of your district. I am an optimist who is convinced that every child can learn.

I believe the public owns the schools, and the superintendent is hired to educate their children. As a result, I seek input from the public and invite community members into the schools. In addition, I inform the public about school activities through press releases, monthly newsletters, and local newspapers. I seek opportunities to speak to civic groups about the excitement of educating kids. I have taken part in establishing a Student Parent Teacher Association, a Parent Advisory Council, and a Booster Club. By being involved in community activities such as the Chamber of Commerce, the Lions Club, my church, and local veterans organizations, I was available to the community.

The superintendent is the educational leader of the district. A good leader earns respect through honesty, caring, and being open. A good leader involves as many people as possible in the decision making process and willingly delegates responsibility. To effect change, the staff must be given the opportunity to provide input. Last year, we completed an extensive, state-mandated Self-Study in three buildings and easily received accreditation. The Study combined input from staff, community members, and students and resulted in a strategic planning session between the board and administrators and in goal setting at the building level. I have established an administrative management team in which all principals are members and have input in management decisions. I participated in building-based management long before it became a buzzword. I have a genuine commitment to education and keep current with educational issues through attendance at workshops, conferences, and graduate studies and by reading professional journals.

I acquired reorganization skills in the military and refined those skills in public education. We established a five-year cycle of curriculum review on a K-12 basis and developed inservice and technology committees to help decide how to improve teaching. The attitude of staff should be to expect the best from kids and that every child is capable of learning. I have helped improve each school district I have served. The bottom line in decision making should always be "Is it best for kids?" Although an agent of change, I was promoted from teacher to principal in Johnson Hole and from principal to superintendent in Georgewood. In both instances, I was strongly supported by staff and community.

Board/superintendent relations are important to the smooth operation of the school district. I am a firm believer the board is responsible for setting policy, and the superintendent is responsible for managing the district. Communication between the board and superintendent is a two-way street. A partnership between the two is absolutely essential. I make a practice of regularly contacting all board members and personally delivering board meeting packets a week before each meeting. In addition, when something unexpected or unusual happens, I inform ALL the board members.

As superintendent in Georgewood I have increased the reserve fund from six percent to fourteen percent of the budget while improving educational offerings. During my tenure, we reduced classified staff and added certificated staff. I wrote grant applications that resulted in additional funding for at-risk students and anti-drug and security programs for K-12. With two other superintendents in neighboring districts, I spearheaded the establishment of a cooperative, resulting in a computer-based Alternative Center for at-risk students, English as a Second Language students, and high school drop-outs. The center, located off campus, was paid for with funds from three separate grants. I have been involved in eight separate successful school levy elections—some as high as 95% passage. A skilled negotiator, I have never had a problem with union negotiations while maintaining prudent use of district funds.

I had overall responsibility for facilities' maintenance for ten years. During that period, I made detailed studies of functions and reorganized maintenance staff to get maximum output. I believe preventative maintenance saves the district money in the long run. The students and staff need a happy and safe place to work and study. I have been involved in two building construction programs and the growth of two school districts.

Experiences in the military and public education prepare me for the diverse population of Cripple Creek. Contacts with military establishments produced the following for my districts: A tank and helicopter brought on campus for students to visit; VIP student tours of the local army and air force bases; speakers at high school assemblies; and erection of light poles for a football field by the National Guard.

In summary, I have experience dealing with the public and staff; the willingness to maintain a broad educational background; the alertness, concern, vision, energy, dedication, and the problem solving skills you are looking for in a superintendent. I have the ability to lead the Cripple Creek School District from an excellent to an exceptional place for kids and employees to reach their highest potential. My university Placement File is en route to you. I look forward to an interview to discuss my qualifications.

Respectfully,

Joseph A. Cool
Enclosures:

Application form
Résumé

It is apparent from the *challenges* and *qualifications* brochure that the school board in Cripple Creek is looking for someone who is a "people person," Someone who is visible in the community and relates well with students and staff. The individual should have a strong background in curriculum and experience in school finance. The candidate must have the ability to manage a growing, diverse community.

Notice that the cover letter addresses the *challenges* and *qualifications* of the Cripple Creek brochure in general terms. Some candidates have listed the *challenges* and *qualifications* in bold print, with their experiences outlined below the sub headings.

There is no right or wrong way. I choose to mix them together so that the letter "flows" better; however you may be sure *someone* in the district will read the cover letter carefully to check if the candidate addresses *all* of the *challenges* and *qualifications*.

The letter calls attention to the students, staff, and community several times. You never know who will be reading your paper. It is important that you address your concerns to all of the patrons of the district.

Be sure to state your college placement file is en route. When you contact the placement file service, verify your file is updated and all the forms and letters current. As I stated earlier, wait two weeks, then contact the school district to be sure they received your placement file. Remember that they put erasers on pencils because people make mistakes.

The *qualifications* and *challenges* will be slightly different for a vice principal or a principal position. A teacher with no administration experience must emphasize her beliefs and leadership styles and show potential.

If you are a vice principal looking for a job as a principal or principal looking for a job as a principal in a larger school or a superintendent job, don't be afraid to assume credit for accomplishments in your building. After all, if you were not there, maybe the school would not have been as successful.

Whether we want to believe it or not, hiring biases exist, and you should be aware of them and work to counteract them. Research from *How To Land The Best Jobs In School Administration,* by Georgia Kosmoski, indicated the following biases:

- Males are usually preferred over females, but this gap has narrowed in recent years.
- When both candidates are highly capable, the job usually goes to the youngest.
- Attractive applicants are usually the choice over unattractive people.
- The mature-faced person is preferred over the baby-faced.

Unlike "General Job" applications, use a paper clip to keep the pages of the letter together, not a staple. Then use a larger paper clip to keep the letter, district application form, and résumé together. This will make it easier for the human resources secretary who may be required to make twenty-five packets for the screening and interview committees.

Before moving on, another reminder is that more is better when sending a cover letter. It should be more than one page and must cover all of the *qualifications* and *challenges* stated in the brochure. A wiser person than I said, "If you don't blow your own horn, someone will come along and hit you over the head with it."

Important Points

1. The cover letter is your only chance to make a good first impression.
2. Keep it simple, but more is better.
3. Get a copy of the school or districts vacancy brochure and study their challenges and desired qualifications.
4. If no brochure is available, call the Human Resources director and get the information.
5. Address all of the challenges and qualifications in your cover letter.
6. It is appropriate to provide the same information in the cover letter as the résumé.
7. Convince the reader that you are the candidate that:
   · Has the ability for the job.
   · Is willing to work long hours and take the bad with the good.
   · Has problem solving skills.
   · Can respond positively to corrective criticism.
   · Supports staff and community.
8. When writing about students, use the synonym "kids"—it's warmer.
9. Make your cover letter interesting. Like a magazine article, convince the reader that the next paragraph will be more interesting.
10. If they use a search consultant, contact her and get the details of the hiring process.
11. Be friendly and respectful when dealing with employees.
12. Use simple white bond paper.
13. The letter should be free of mistakes.
14. Use paper clips, not staples.

You have their interest. Now you have to maintain it with a good application form. It sounds easier than it is. What can be more boring than a form?

Chapter Three

The Ubiquitous Application Form

I have never been able to figure out exactly why every school district has administrator candidates complete an application form. I can understand why for other school employees, but not administrators.

When you see the vacancy announcement, call the contact person at the school district and ask for the paperwork requirements. If the staff member mentions a district application form, ask her to mail a copy to you.

If the district is within driving distance, offer to stop by and pick up the form. It will give you an opportunity to make a favorable impression on the human resources secretary and get some answers to your questions.

Part of the application procedure in some districts is to complete an application form electronically. They use this initial electronic form to screen applicants, then they ask the remaining candidates to complete and submit a cover letter and résumé.

Almost all of the information asked for on the standard application form is found in the candidate's college placement file. The only reason I can see for the requirement is for legal leverage.

Every application form has statements such as:

1. "Have you ever been arrested for anything more serious than a traffic violation?"
2. "By signing this form you are certifying that everything on it truthful."

If you are hired, and they discover you provided false information on the form, it gives them grounds for termination. Be careful to complete every box on the application form and that it is accurate.

I have seen many employees terminated for falsifying an application form. More and more school districts are requiring finger printing and background checks by the police.

For several years, I sat on a teacher certification appeals board for the state superintendent's office. I recall a case where a teacher lost his job and teaching certificate for falsifying an application form.

He indicated that he had not been arrested for anything more serious than a traffic violation, but during a background check, they found he had been arrested 22 years earlier at age 19 for breaking into a snack bar. He pled guilty, paid a fine, and did community service, with the promise that his records would be expunged after two years.

Obviously, someone in the police department forgot to expunge the records. Fortunately, the teacher not only had a very competent lawyer but a fair-minded group of educators on the appeals committee, and we overturned the punishment.

If you were arrested several years ago, I suggest that you contact the police department or court system and try to get the arrest cleared from your record. If unsuccessful, be sure to list it on the district application form. It might eliminate you from consideration, but it may also be overlooked. If so, once you are hired, you may be able to explain the details of the arrest to the satisfaction of your employer.

The application form will closely resemble the placement file historical document. When you update your placement file, make a photocopy of the historical document. You can use it to complete the district application form. Good screening committees compare the two forms for inconsistencies.

The key words in filling out the application form are neatness, accuracy, and completeness. Do not use a pencil or pen—you might as well use a *crayon*.

Look around until you find a good typewriter. Do not try to duplicate the form on your computer—unless you can make it exactly the same. Some people object to the forms being reproduced.

Photocopy the form and type it first on the copied form to be sure that what you want to say fits into those pesky little boxes. Once you make the adjustments, go ahead and type it onto the original form.

Under the list of educational institutions you attended, be sure to list them all—even if you only took one course. If a screener finds out you attended a college that you did not list, it sends up a red flag that could easily eliminate you. There are usually so many applicants for administrative jobs that part of the process is to eliminate applicants along the way and interview those still standing.

Be accurate with your grade point average because your placement file may contain your transcripts, and the GPA is listed. The district may send for your college transcripts and check the GPA.

The districts usually ask you to list previous employment in reverse chronological order. If so, make sure you have them in order and do not leave any out. A member of the screening committee, a consultant or one of the district staff will probably contact all of your previous places of employment. They will always ask the following questions.

Questions Asked About You

- What were the dates of your employment?
- What was your job and the name of your supervisor?
- Why did you leave?

They will also contact your supervisors, ask them about your job performance, and the reason that you left. Sometimes they will contact other employees in the school or district to find out how you related to people that were not your direct supervisor.

There is always a little box that asks the reason you left each job. Be sure that you are accurate. If you departed by mutual consent, say that. If you say that you left to pursue other options and they find out that your district chose not to renew your contract, your file will probably be shredded.

Remember back in Chapter One I talked about character references? This is where some of them are listed.

Character References

- Pick good character references.
- Ask their permission.
- Prep them with responses that will help you get the job.

In "general jobs," employers might want character references like clergy, neighbors, or friends. School consultants are looking for people that can talk about how well you performed your job, how well you related to other people, and how well you related to kids. They are still interested in some community members, however.

When I applied for a position as a high school principal, I listed:

1. A school board member because he had been instrumental in promoting me from teacher to principal.
2. A principal that I had worked with in the district.
3. A judge who had a child who attended my school.

I helped them by providing the names and phone numbers of other people the inquirer could contact that might know me. Since I provided the names, I was sure they would have favorable things to say.

There is no point in listing former supervisors or people who wrote letters of recommendation for your placement file. That information is already available to them. Remember you are trying to provide *more* people that will say nice things about you.

Another reminder that you check either the "yes" or "no" box after the question, "Have you ever been arrested for anything more serious than a traffic violation?" A friend missed the boxes, and an assistant superintendent called him and asked him why the box was not checked. My friend apologized and told him that he had inadvertently missed the boxes. He requested that the form be returned to him so that it could be completed. The administrator sent the form back, and my friend resubmitted but did not receive an interview.

Would you believe that I have seen numerous application forms that were submitted unsigned? Would you believe that none of them got an interview? Remember to sign the form.

After you have checked the completed form against your historical document in your placement file, have your spouse or a good friend do the same thing. Four eyes are better than two.

Important Points

1. The application form can hurt you as much as it can help you.
2. Be sure it is complete, accurate, and neat.
3. Be sure the information on the application form corresponds to the data on the historical document in your college placement file.
4. If you have been arrested—even as a juvenile—check to see if there is a record. If so, try to have the record expunged.
5. If an arrest record cannot be expunged, be sure to list it on the application form.
6. List all educational institutes attended.
7. List all previous employment.
8. Pick good character references, and prep them with good things to say about you. Give the search committee names, telephone numbers, and addresses of others that will say good things about you. Make sure these people are not the people who wrote letters of recommendation for you.
9. Double and triple check the form to be sure it is accurate and complete.
10. Be sure to sign the form.

That chore completed, attach a paper clip to your cover letter and set it aside. It is time to tackle your résumé!

Chapter Four

What About the Résumé?

The résumé is the main course of the application packet. It is one of the most important pieces in your application packet. The people involved in the hiring process study it carefully. Expect it to be read and re-read.

Once again, the résumé for a school administrator is entirely different from "general jobs." This is my *third* reminder that more is better. You are encouraged to have more than a one-page résumé. In some circles, the résumé is even referred to as a "curriculum vita" or CV. The title even sounds longer, doesn't it?

It should go without saying that you are honest in formulating your résumé, but we have all heard or experienced someone who embellished their accomplishments. Honesty is an important quality required of all school administrators.

Will a "knockout" résumé guarantee you a job? No, but it could get you an interview that could get you a job. Keep in mind that you are trying to separate yourself from the pack.

A good résumé must be inspiring. It must move the reader to take action. Most people see a résumé as being a chronological history of their lives, including work and education history and interests. Their résumés reflect just that, and they wonder why they don't get interviews. "After all," they ask themselves, "Aren't I the most qualified?" They may be, but the reader doesn't get far enough into the résumé to find out.

Your résumé must be an exciting paper that:

- Is produced using the proper combination of paper, ink, and equipment to demonstrate your professional likeness.
- Follows the simple rules of good résumé writing. They include: outward form, action words, proper punctuation, spelling, correct grammar, and different specifications.
- Communicates a sense of vision, ability, honesty, enthusiasm, energy, and likeability.
- Connects your unique skills, experience, and interest to the employer's needs.

The *purpose* of writing, producing, and distributing a résumé is simply to get a job interview. No big secret, right? In that case, you should only include those details that are of interest to employers. What do they want to see? They want to see sound evidence of *your probable future performance* and how you will fit in as a leader in their school or school district. It is not just a summary of your work and education history.

Remember employers are betting on your future, but your pattern of performance can usually predict future achievement. Your résumé should be a way for you to tell the reader that you have the "all-star" ability to fit her particular needs.

The methods you use in résumé writing reflect how you view yourself in relation to employers. If you merely list your work history, you are likely to present a self-centered image that says nothing about your interests, skills, and abilities in relation to the needs of the employer. If your résumé is not "employer oriented," it will probably end up in the shredder.

However, if you thoughtfully review the *challenges and qualifications* listed in the vacancy brochure and relate your skills and accomplishments to them, you should produce a résumé that surpasses your history as it clearly communicates your qualifications to the reader.

This is an *employer-centered* résumé and it will separate you from the pack and get you that interview.

A winning résumé

- Immediately impresses the reader.
- Is visually attractive and easy to read.
- Focuses on the employer's needs.
- Communicates your job-related abilities and patterns of performance.
- Stresses your leadership ability and potential for solving school problems.
- Communicates that you are a responsible, honest, and a genuine person.

A losing résumé

- *Has poor format and outward appearance.* This person doesn't care enough about herself to read a book on résumé writing and understand the importance.
- *Have misspellings, bad grammar, punctuation, lengthy phrases, and wordiness.* If she can't communicate in writing, how can I expect her to communicate with staff, students, and community members?
- *Is poorly typed and reproduced.* I don't think this person respects me enough to give me a quality product.
- *Is too slick, and gimmicky.* Pink paper? Please! A manipulator is just what we need around here.
- *Is too boastful or dishonest.* I've been there before. I'll spend all my time separating truth from fiction.
- *Has irrelevant information.* Is it really important that you were a member of your high school cheerleading team?
- *Is missing categories.* Any special awards or recognition? Participation in community activities?
- *Has unexplained time gaps.* What did she do between 1985–87? A prison sentence?
- *Is hard to understand or interpret.* I have read all this "stuff," and I still don't know what she can do.

• *Does not convey accomplishments or pattern of performance from which reader can predict future performance.* An interesting life, but I still don't know what this person can do for this school district.

Writing the résumé

The school administrator résumé usually includes:

• *Individual contact information.* This is necessary and should be at the top of the résumé. Name recognition is important. I recommend your name be in large bold print at the top of the page.
• *Education.* List in reverse chronological order the dates of attendance, names of colleges, and degrees.
• *Professional work experience.* Provide only work experience related to school—unless it is an outstanding leadership job. For example, while in college, for two years you coordinated work experience jobs on campus. This is the most important part of your résumé. This is where you can tie in your work experience with the *challenges and qualifications* that the hiring district is looking for. It bears repeating that this is not just a list. It is a series of short sentences that catapults your life history into action. Your résumé should show potential employers that you have been super-charged and are a person of action. Do so by starting every sentence with one of the words in the table on the following page. Each job you had should have a series of cryptic, descriptive accomplishments. For example, "*Created* a hands-on math curriculum that was adopted district-wide." Emphasize results as much as possible.

Résumé Action Words

Achieved	Employed	Organized
Adapted	Equipped	Performed
Advised	Established	Persuaded
Analyzed	Evaluated	Planned
Assisted	Expanded	Processed
Built	Experienced	Produced
Completed	Generated	Rectified
Controlled	Guided	Reduced
Convinced	Handled	Researched
Coordinated	Identified	Served
Counseled	Improved	Set up
Created	Initiated	Sold
Decided	Learned	Strengthened
Delivered	Led	Supervised
Designed	Maintained	Taught
Developed	Managed	Trained
Directed	Operated	Wrote

Research from *How to Land The Best Jobs In School Administration*, by Georgia Kosmoski, has shown that there are pre-existing notions about gender weaknesses. They are as follows:

Men

- Lack of knowledge and experience.
- Don't support the democratic process and discourage collegiality.
- Are weak disciplinarians.
- Are likely to make changes only for change sake.

Women

- Lack strength and are too emotional.
- Are weak disciplinarians.
- Don't have adequate experience.
- Don't support collegiality.

Therefore in this section it behooves both genders to emphasize:
- A commitment to firm discipline.
- A wide range of public relations experience.
- A positive attitude.
- Very knowledgeable, with good problem solving skills.

Further, other areas of importance you should emphasize in this section are:

- Student and staff safety.
- Test results/accountability.
- Cultural diversity and civility programs.

Professional recognition. Teacher of the Year, Principal of the County, Most Humane Superintendent, etc.

Community activities. President of the Lions Club, member of American Legion, Vice President of Chamber of Commerce.

Volunteer positions held. President of Georgewood High School curriculum committee. Vice President of Georgewood High School Education Association. Member Georgewood site based committee.

Honors and awards. Teacher of the Year, Georgewood School District, Man of the Year, Slowpoke Chamber of Commerce. Woman of the Year, Los Angeles Times.

Certification. List certification in reverse chronological order. 1995, Superintendents credentials, 1986; Principals credentials, 1979; teachers certificate, grades 7–12.

Publications. Article published, *The Changing Principalship,* "American Association of Secondary School Principals," Jun 1998.

Foreign language. List only if it is relevant to the job being pursued. If the building or district has a large Hispanic population, it would be appropriate to note if you speak Spanish.

Hobbies and interests. Enjoy reading books about school leadership (this indicates that you study your profession in your spare time). Also enjoy swimming, jogging, and bicycling, and like to keep physically fit (especially if you are in your 50s or 60s and want to portray an active, physically fit leader). Obviously, you do not use this category if you are a workaholic or don't have a life.

Military experience. This should be listed under work experience. Always try to point out leadership experience. 1990–1992, US Army Sergeant. Was a combat squad leader, commanding 10 men during the battle for Kuwait. Decorations: Bronze Star for Valor and Purple Heart. (It indicates that you were a leader under difficult circumstances and received a decoration for your actions.)

Personal data. Use this only if information you have will be helpful: Married, with four school age-children. (If you are applying in a small district that has problems with student population growth, your family could help balance their budget.)

References. Even though your college placement file and application forms usually have character references or letters of recommendation, I like to list references. It provides an opportunity to furnish names of other people that will "sing your praises."

The question invariably arises, "Should I put a goal or objective on the résumé?" It is not necessary for school administrators because your cover letter shows the job for which you are applying. If the two papers get separated, the fact that the résumé is in a pile of applications for a high school principal job opening should indicate that the résumé is for that vacancy.

Types of résumés

There are two general types of résumés: The *chronological* and the *functional*. If you are in a situation where any of the following has occurred, you may want to opt for the *functional* format:

- Lack experience in the job.
- Made a lateral move or a move back to a position of less responsibility.
- Had a period of unemployment.
- Have a record of job hopping.
- Are nearing retirement age.

In the *functional* format you explain what you have done according to job function or type of work performed. Group related successes together regardless of the district in which they occurred. At the end of the résumé, create a section titled, *Employment History* and list in reverse chronological order, the names of employers, their locations, and dates of employment. Including job titles is optional.

Disadvantages of the functional format

Some consultants know that one of the purposes of this format is to conceal liabilities. They may have used it themselves.

Some employers don't like to read functional résumés because it is difficult to tell with which school district, accomplishments and duties occurred.

You should weigh the extent of the problem areas that you are trying to overcome against strengths of your qualifications. As a general rule, the more serious the liabilities, the more you will need to use the *functional* approach. Your strong experiences and job skills will work to offset these problem areas.

The *chronological* format places emphasis on titles, dates, and places of employment. It emphasizes when you did something and what you accomplished. This might accent your problem areas.

Educators who want to move to a first principal or superintendent job should use a heading called *Qualified By* to tie-in their qualifications to the hiring districts announced *challenges and qualifications*. These should be used at the beginning of the résumé as an attention grabber.

Important Points

1. Keep it simple.
2. Stress your achievements.
3. Exude enthusiasm.
4. Be honest and don't boast.
5. Use as many specific examples as possible
6. Tie the résumé to the needs of the job.
7. Individualize for the job.
8. Use simple everyday language.
9. Do not limit to one or two pages.
10. Keep the sentences short.
11. Use single-line bullet entries.
12. Highlight section headings.
13. Single space within sections.
14. Double space between sections.
15. Do not write in paragraphs.
16. Use white paper.
17. Use 8 1/2 by 11–inch paper.

18. Use white areas of the page to break-up writing.
19. Purchase quality copies.
20. Correct the spelling.
21. Re-do it if it is sloppy.
22. Don't mention the salary.

Draft your résumé on a computer. That way you can make adjustments for each application. Most copy shops can print your résumé from a floppy disk. Now let's move on to personalizing your résumé.

Chapter Five

Personalize Your Résumé

Now we know what goes into a résumé, so let's personalize yours. Select a résumé format that best conveys your experience, skills, and future performance. It will depend on your own unique qualifications and qualities.

On the following pages are four sample résumés based on the sample *challenges and qualifications* used in the *Cover Letter* in Chapter Two. Note how the qualifications and experiences of the candidates jump off the page and mesh with the requirements of the hiring district. I have used the *chronological* format for the samples.

Ms. Henrieta Hot who is currently a *teacher*, and is applying for a job as a *high school vice principal.*

Mr. Samuel Swift is a *vice principal* and is applying for a job as *principal of a large high school.*

Dr. Irvin Smart is a high school *principal* and is looking for a job as *superintendent of a small to medium sized district.*

Dr. Brenda Bright is currently a *superintendent* and is looking for a job as *superintendent of a larger school district.*

Lets review how they packaged their résumés to get an interview.

Ms. Hot's résumé is at Sample 1.

She has no previous experience as an administrator. Her strengths are in her two masters' degrees and certification, so those are placed near the front of her résumé. But she needs an attention grabber. Right after her name, she demonstrates to her potential employer that she has the qualifications to merit a second look.

She was fortunate to have been the acting principal of the high school for a few months. During that time she was able to accomplish some tasks that fit well with the hiring district's needs. Her two-year internship allowed her to garner some valuable experience as well.

Research has shown that women are perceived as soft on discipline, so she expresses that she administered even-handed discipline. Henrieta provides evidence that she learned from being on the Accreditation team and from being a member of the hiring team.

Ms. Hot indicates that as a teacher, she sought leadership positions such as department chair, athletic director, coach, president of SPTA, and the chair for several committees. She is not intimidated by a school board because she made several verbal presentations to them.

Ms. Hot listed other employment because it indicates not merely that she worked in higher education but had a responsible job there. Her résumé indicates that while she started out to be interested in business administration, she decided that working with young people was more fulfilling.

Notice that she listed awards. Some districts are impressed by awards. There is no point in getting them if you do not use them. She lists her participation in civic activities and her leadership roles to express her participation with community members and her willingness to take leadership positions. Henrieta lists leadership in professional organizations as well.

Recognizing that her college placement file has character references and letters of recommendation from her supervisors in current and previous jobs, Henrieta decided to list people with whom she worked. This gives the potential employer leads to talk with co-workers. She recognizes people need to be able to get along with co-workers as well. In rare instances, candidates list high school student leaders as character references.

Not many high schools are able to hire vice principals with previous experience. Ms. Hot is taking a logical step and with this résumé, and she should get an interview.

Sample Résumé 1

HENRIETA A. HOT

1234 Castle St.   Home (241) 555–9876
Last Chance, WY 92431   Office (241) 555–1020

Qualified By

- Thirteen Years as Classroom Teacher
- Six months Acting Principal
- Chairman District Curriculum Committee
- Member, District Community Outreach Group

- Requisite Education and Certification
- Proven leadership in ed. and business
- Vice-Chair Building Finance committee
- Completed Two Year Principal Internship

Education

M.A.	University of Wyoming, Cheyenne, Wyoming Most of work in school administration	1998
M.A.	University of Arizona, Tucson, Arizona Majored in Education	1986
B.A.	Arizona State University, Tempe, Arizona Majored in Business Administration	1983

Certification

- Initial Principal Certificate, University of Wyoming   1999
- Continuing Teaching Certificate, 7–12, University of Wyoming   1991
- Initial Teaching Certificate, 7–12, University of Wyoming   1986
- Initial Teaching Certificate, 7–12, Arizona State University   1986

Administrative Experience

Principal

Central High School, Last Chance, Wyoming   *1999*

- Took over leadership for Principal who was out on long term illness.
- Led the school through a difficult Accreditation process.

· Established the largest teacher library in the state.

· Initiated state mandated test—students scored highest in region.

Principal intern

Central High School, Last Chance, Wyoming *1997–99*

· Responsible for even handed student discipline for grades 9 and 10.

Henrieta Hot

Page 2

· Principal's representative to the student council.

· Managed and balanced the school's budget.

· Organized and led the school's accreditation team.

· Established inservice program for staff to prepare students for state mandated testing.

· Supervised a student-led cultural diversity club that was the model for other schools.

· Supervised extracurricular activities.

· Member of interview committee for staff hiring.

Teaching Experience

Central High School, Last Chance, Wyoming *1989–99*

· Taught business classes, grades 9–12.

· Coached varsity soccer and softball nine years, winning two state championships.

· Directed all athletics for five years.

· Led the business department for seven years.

· President, SPTA three years.

· Initiated DECA program for the school. Chapter received national recognition.

· Charter member of school's site based management team.

· Took leadership role in school community relation's team.

· Chair of district curriculum revision team to align with state requirements.

· Chair of student athletic and attendance appeals committee.

· Co-chair of district teacher in-service committee.

· Made numerous verbal presentations to District School Board.

· *Northern High School, Cheyenne, Wyoming* *1986–89*

· Taught business classes, grades 9–12.

· Coached varsity track and girls basketball.

· Established the technology program in the school.

· Sponsor of Native American club.

Henrieta A. Hot

Page 3

Other Employment Experience

University of Arizona Athletic Department, Tucson, Arizona   *1983–86*

· Assistant to marketing director in University Athletic Director's office.
· Responsible for advertisement and ticketing of all home athletic events.

Awards

· Teacher of the Year, State of Wyoming	1998
· Citizen of the Year, Last Chance Chamber of Commerce	1997

Civic Activities

· President and coach, Last Chance Girls' Softball Association.
· Member, Last Chance Chamber of Commerce.
· Vice-president, Last Chance Lions Club.

Professional Organizations

· President, Last Chance Teachers Association.
· Vice President, Wyoming State Athletic Director's Association.
· American Association of Secondary School Principals.
· Wyoming Association of Secondary School Principals.

References

Mrs. Barbara Tell, President, Last Chance Education Association E-mail, btell@lchance.ed	(241) 555–9641
Mr. Ben Down, Custodian, Central High School, Last Chance, Wyoming E-mail, bdown@lchance.ed	(241) 555–1025
Mr. Hal Backus, Athletic Director, Central High School, Last Chance, Wyoming E-mail, hbackus@lchance.ed	(241) 555–1030

Mr. Samuel Swift is a vice principal and wants to make the logical move to building principal.

His résumé is at Sample 2. Swift has excellent experience as an administrator in a large high school. His attention grabber is his experience as an administrator. In today's market, experienced principals of large high schools are hard to find. Most employers are looking for people with leadership experience in high schools. Mr. Swift is in the second tier of the group, right after current building principals.

His résumé exhibits the connection with his experience and the *challenges and qualifications* needs of the hiring district. He illustrates that he personally supervised 50 teachers. Some building principals do not supervise that many staff. Further, he points out that in the absence of the building principal, he is in charge. He shows the principal has confidence in his leadership abilities.

He indicates concrete examples of experience. For example, the hiring district wants someone with interest and experience in cultural diversity. Mr. Swift "established and supervised a cultural diversity club." His résumé expresses that he worked in three culturally diverse school districts and was successful.

His certification paragraph shows he has a principal certificate. The Teacher of the Year award from a citizen's group indicates that he was involved with the community. It ties in well with the participation and leadership in both civic and professional organizations.

His publications not only demonstrate an interest in writing, which is always looked on favorably by employers, but both school safety and Spanish language subjects are "hot buttons."

Mr. Swift must have had a special relationship with the current superintendent, so he listed him as a character reference. Employers are impressed when they have lower level administrators working with the superintendent. Moreover, if the vice chair of the school board is listed, that will impress employers. By listing the president of the teacher's union, Mr. Swift is showing that he has developed a good relationship with the union. Sometimes that is not possible when one serves on the negotiation team and must make difficult decisions about teacher assignments.

Sample Résumé 2

SAMUEL I. SWIFT

2468 North St.
Nothing, CA 92167

Home (301) 555–6756
Office (301) 555–9182

Administrative Experience

Vice Principal

Bayview High School, Monterey, California

1996–99

- 2,000 students, with 12% minority, grades 9–12.
- 150 certificated and 150 classified staff.
- During the last year was acting principal during absence of principal.
- Committed to firm discipline for 600 students.
- Responsible for school public relations overall.
- Supervised 50 certificated and 30 classified employees.
- Wrote and executed security and disaster plans for the school.
- Chair of five-year curriculum review cycle committee.
- Responsible for school testing—test scores improved by nine percentile points in three years.
- Chair of building budget committee that maintained a balanced budget.
- Wrote grant requests resulting in $150,000.00 in computer hardware.
- Directed all athletic programs for the school, supervising over 100 coaches.
- Established and supervised a cultural diversity club.
- Served on district labor negotiation team.

Teaching Experience

- East Central High School, Los Angeles, California

1986–96

- 1,600 students, 45% Hispanic.
- Completed a two-year principal internship.
- Taught Spanish and English as a Second Language.
- Coached varsity football. Won the city championship four years.

Samual A. Swift

Page 2 East Central High (Continued)

· Initiated and chairperson of staff cultural diversity committee.
· Established and chaired student appeals committee.
· Designed and coordinated a parent newsletter that received statewide recognition.
· Chairperson of the building budget that was always in balance.
· Served on the foreign language curriculum adoption committee.

West Salinas High School, Salinas, California   *1983–86*

· 900 students, 35% minority.
· Taught Spanish and English as a Second Language (ESL).
· Assistant coach, football and baseball.
· Wrote a federal grant resulting in $50,000.00 for technology.
· Established a Spanish language computer program for ESL students.

Education

M.A.	University of California at Los Angeles, Los Angeles, California	1995
	All of courses in education administration	
B.A.	University of California, Berkeley, California	1983

Certification

· Continuing Principal Certificate, University of California at Los Angeles 1999
· Initial Principal Certificate, University of California at Los Angeles 1995
· Continuing Teaching Certificate, University of California 1987
· Initial Teaching Certificate, University of California 1983

Awards

· Administrator of the Year, Monterey School District 1999
· Teacher of the Year, Hispanic Citizens Alliance, Los Angeles, CA 1991

Civic Activities

· President of Our Saviors Lutheran Church.
· Secretary, Monterey Chamber of Commerce.
· Member, Salinas City improvement committee.
· Member, Los Angeles Sunrise Kiwanis Club.

Samuel A Swift
Page 3 (continued)

Publications

· *School Safety a Must*, American Association of Secondary School Principals' Association, October '97.
· *Spanish to English, or English to Spanish, Which is Best?* Journal of American Educators, June '90.

Professional Organizations

· Member, National Association of Secondary School Principals.
· Member, California Association of Secondary School Principals.
· Member, National Education Association.
· President, Los Angeles Education Association

References

Dr. Chauncie Misselhut, Superintendent, Monterey School District   (301) 555–3040
E-mail, cmisselhut@monterey.ed.ca
Ms. Priscilla Pueterbucket, President, Monterey Education Association   (301) 555–3141
E-mail, ppueterbucket@monterey.ed.ca
Mr. Justin Tyme, Vice Chair, Monterey School District Board of Education   (301) 555–3000
E-mail, jtyme@monterey.ed.ca

Dr. Irvin Smart is at Sample Résumé 3.

He is currently a principal of a fairly large high school and aspires to be a *superintendent.* Some people are impressed by people with a doctorate. Dr. Smart recognized, however, that he needed to get the attention of the potential employer. He therefore listed the qualifications that matched the hiring district's *challenges and qualifications.*

Smart used action verbs to illustrate his leadership style, interest in involving the community, and ability to balance a budget while improving learning in the schools. Everyone is looking for cultural diversity and improved test scores. If one does not indicate improved test scores, it leaves the reader to assume that test scores did not improve.

He showed he was a change agent by "initiating team teaching in the building." With the importance of passing levy and bond elections, Smarts participation with the campaign committee was…umm…smart.

Dr. Smart dropped out of the work force to pursue his Ph.D. He did not want to show a gap in employment, so he listed "Graduate Assistant 1989–91," under work. He can do that because technically most doctorate candidates work for the university under a work study program.

Smart indicated under his teaching experience that he developed a cultural diversity council and was involved in public relations. This demonstrates a pattern of involvement and helps the reader evaluate future potential.

Smart already has a superintendent certificate. The current certificate eliminates a reason for a consultant to place his employment packet at the bottom of the pile.

Receiving an award from the Seattle Lions Club is evidence Smart is deeply involved in community activities. Even though Smart listed "president of Seattle Sunset Lions Club," consultants recognize that some civic presidents do little more then preside at monthly meetings.

Being a leader in every civic activity is proof Smart seeks responsibility and recognizes the importance of community involvement. Even though the titles of the published articles are not impressive, the fact that Smart wrote them helps to separate him from the pack.

Under character references, Smart listed an assistant superintendent that is not his supervisor. He is giving the reader an opportunity to talk to a co-worker. Ms. O'Hare, the superintendent of Pasco School District, is intriguing. A consultant will call her just out of curiosity (and Smart knows she will have nice things to say about him).

Smart must have had a special relationship with the president of a big city school district classified union. He can tell the consultant a great deal about Smart's leadership style and what classified employees in Smart's building think of him.

Sample Résumé 3

IRVIN M. SMART

12361 Hillside Avenue
Seattle, WA 98301

Home (206) 555–9080
Office (206) 555–1918

Qualified By

· Proven dedication to excellence in education
· Built team concept in building leadership
· Generated cultural diversity in four schools
· Have a collaborative leadership style
· Experience in grades K–12

· Actively involved in community activities
· Interest in education and safety of children
· Achieved a balanced budget in two schools
· Encouraged community support of school
· strategic planning

Education

Ph.D.	Washington State University, Pullman, Washington Education Administration	1991
M.A.	Washington State University, Pullman, Washington Half of courses in school administration	1985
B.S.	Gonzaga, University, Spokane, Washington Majored in Science and elementary education	1979

Administrative Experience

Principal

Hillview High School, Seattle, Washington   1994–99

· 1200 students with 25% minority, grades 9–12.
· 75 certificated and 65 classified staff.
· Initiated site based management in the school.
· Produced a balanced budget five straight years while improving course offerings.
· Established a community outreach committee to receive input from parents.
· Improved standardized test scores by 10 percentile points.
· Generated inservice for staff to initiate state mandated testing for 10th graders.
· Showed improvement in 10th grade testing.

- Taught parenting class to parents of at-risk 9th grade students.
- Created a safety plan for students and staff.
- Persuaded the central office to hire two security officers.
- Guided the school through an accreditation process.

Irvin M. Smart

Page 2

Parkside Middle School, Seattle, Washington   *1991–94*

- 600 students with 40% minority, grades 5–6.
- 22 certificated and 23 classified staff.
- Initiated team teaching in the building.
- Improved standardized test scores by 15 percentile points.
- Established a parent advisory committee for decision making process.
- Employed a staff consensus decision making process for major decisions.
- Achieved a balanced budget and improved curriculum every year.
- Developed and edited a monthly newsletter that was sent to all parents.
- Led a large part of the district Maintenance and Operations campaign committee.
- Planned, coordinated, and managed the opening of a new school building.

Graduate Assistant

Washington State University, Pullman, Washington   1989–91

- Worked for Dean of Education while pursuing Doctorate degree.
- Assisted professors with classes and grading of papers.
- Coordinated training sessions for College of Education staff.

Teaching Experience

Central Junior High School, Pullman, Washington   1985–89

- Taught 7–9th grade science.
- Developed and supervised a cultural diversity council for the school.
- Organized a positive drug prevention program.

Valley Intermediate School, Richland, Washington   1979–85

- Taught 5th and 6th grade block classes in science and mathematics.
- Organized input from the staff and produced the weekly parents newsletter.

Certification

- Initial Superintendent Certificate, University of Washington — 1999
- Continuing Principal Certificate, K-12, Washington State University — 1995
- Initial Principal Certificate, K-12, Washington State University — 1990

Irvin M. Smart

Page 3 Certification (Continued)

- Continuing Teaching Certificate K-12, Washington State University — 1984
- Initial Teaching Certificate, K-12, Gonzaga University — 1979

Awards

- Principal of the Year, Seattle School District — 1994
- Lion of the Year, Seattle Sunset Lions Club — 1996

Civic Activities

- President, St. Paul's Church council.
- President, Seattle Sunset Lions Club.
- President, South Seattle Little League Baseball Association.
- Scoutmaster, Southside Seattle Boy Scouts of America.

Publications

- *What is a Doctorate Worth?* National Association of Secondary School Principals' Magazine, January '95.
- Has Science Curriculum Improved Since the Walk on the Moon? National Association of Secondary School Principals' Magazine, April '94.

Professional Organizations

- Washington Association of School Administrators
- American Association of Secondary School Principals
- Washington Association of Secondary School Principals
- National Education Association
- Washington Education Association

References

Mr. Ben Crazy, Asst. Superintendent, Seattle School District   (206) 555–7656
E-mail, bcrazy@seattlesd.educ

Ms. Sandra O'Hare, Superintendent, Pasco School District   (509) 555–6968
E-mail, sohare@pasco.ed
Mr. Keith Kleen, President, Seattle School District Classified Union   (206) 555–5051
E-mail, kkleen@seattlesd.educ

Dr. Brenda Bright is a current superintendent that wants to move to a larger school district.

Her résumé at Sample 4 is carefully written so her experience, education, and potential obviously match the *challenges and qualifications* advertised by the hiring district. She went to great lengths to illustrate that she has been a success at every job she has tackled—and no job is too big for her.

Her wide range of job experience is a double edge sword, however. On the one hand, she has a rich background; on the other, she shows a pattern of not staying in one place very long. If she was a principal and showed a continued pattern of moving, it would be detrimental.

In her case, she is a superintendent, and they do not usually last more than five years in one place. She has shown a logical progression from being a principal of a small elementary school to a large junior high school. Then she moved on to be a superintendent.

It appears that she did course work on her Ph.D. while working in Spokane, then took a year off work to meet campus residence requirements. She made that quite clear in her résumé, so the gap in employment did not raise a red flag.

Dr. Bright skillfully indicates she is a "rising star" from her selection to replace a principal in mid-year to success in two other school buildings and a successful tenure as superintendent. Further evidence is in the number of awards from community groups and professional organizations.

In her list of publications, she gives the reader a chance to ask how she "picked up" the school in mid-year during her first stint as a principal. Her other articles are also of high interest to every school district.

She has so many other items to list on her résumé; it is not necessary to list her "initial" teacher, principal, and superintendent certificates.

Dr. Bright's active membership and leadership in civic and professional organizations at every stop in her career provide evidence she is always involved. It is further evidence she will continue to be involved.

The listing of the vice president of the school board as a character reference indicates she has another supporter on the board. The president has probably already written a letter of recommendation for her placement file. Listing the president of the teacher's union demonstrates she enjoys a good relationship with him. By listing the chief of police, Dr. Bright is not only showing she enjoys a good rapport with the Chief, but she must have worked with him on school safety—a "hot button" these days. I have no doubt her résumé will be at the top of the pile.

Sample Résumé 4

BRENDA A. BRIGHT

9876 Pine Street   Home (509) 555–5434
Medical River, WA 98888   Office (509) 555–8000
E-mail, bbright@medicalr.ed

Administrative Experience:

Superintendent

Medical River School District, Medical River, Washington   1995–99

- 2,700 students, preschool-Grade 12.
- 200 certificated and 190 classified staff.
- Initiated strategic planning committee of staff and community resulting in complete restructuring of schools.
- Improved public relations by getting more community members involved in schools and more staff involved in community activities.
- Introduced site-based management resulting in staff and community involvement in decision-making affecting their building.
- Led a district from financial crisis to one with 5% cash reserve while improving educational programs.
- Reorganized the central office and building administrators to provide a cohesive administrative team.
- Improved standardized test scores by eight percentile points.
- Showed steady improvement in state mandated tests.
- Established a community task force on youth violence resulting in safer conditions in the schools.
- Facilitated, through Chamber of Commerce, only district in the state with a business partner for every school in the district.
- Delivered a K–12 curriculum of cultural diversity and directed inservice training for all staff.
- Lead labor negotiator for the district.
- Assisted in passage of two Maintenance and Operations levy elections and a ten million-dollar building bond election.

Brenda A Bright

Page 2, Medical River (continued)

· Lobbied state legislators for support of schools.

Graduate Assistant

Gonzaga University, Spokane, Washington   1994–95

· Assisted professors in presenting classes to undergraduates.
· Wrote a curriculum for tying teaching curriculum to tests.

Principal

Washington Junior High School, Spokane, Washington   1991–94

· 24 certificated and 18 classified staff.
· Improved public relations by strengthening SPTA.
· Persuaded businesses to support the school by having their employees volunteer in the classrooms.
· Introduced a cooperative management style to the employees and parents.
· Improved 8th grade test scores by ten percentile points in all areas.
· Implemented a school-wide study skills program.
· Instituted a required self esteem class for all 7th graders.
· Taught parenting skills to 7th grade parents.
· *Lincoln Intermediate School*, Prairie Heights, Washington   1987–91
· 500 students, grades 5–6.
· 22 certificated and 15 classified staff.
· Most of student body composed of minority students.
· Improved standardized test scores by 20 percentile points.
· Wrote and supervised federal grants for the district.
· Program director for Title IV-A Indian Education and Chapter I and II.
· Worked with community Maintenance and Operations levy campaign committee.
· Directed racial diversity training for all staff.

King Elementary School, Richville, Washington   1984–87

· 350 students, grades K–6.
· 15 certificated and 10 classified staff.
· Assumed leadership of the school in mid year.

Brenda A. Bright

Page 3, King Elementary (continued)

· Initiated positive school community relations.
· Developed multidisciplinary team for special education students.
· Facilitated inservice training to improve teaching methods.
· Organized scheduled replacement of teaching equipment.
· Improved test scores by 13 percentile points.

Teaching Experience:

King Elementary School, Richville, Washington   1977–84

· Taught grades 4, 5, and 6.
· Introduced use of personal computers in the classroom.

Education:

Ph.D.	*Gonzaga University*, Spokane, Washington Education Administration	1995
M.A.	*Washington State University*, Pullman, Washington All of classes in school administration	1983
B.A.	*University of Washington*, Seattle, Washingto	1977

Awards:

· Superintendent of the Year, Education Service District #100	1999
· Woman of the Year, Medical River League of Women Voters	1998
· Principal of the Year, Spokane School District	1994
· Finalist, Intermediate School Principal of the Year, State of Washington	1991
· Nominee, Principal of the Year, National Association of Elementary School Principals	1987
· Citizen of the Year, Richville Chamber of Commerce	1986

Publications:

· *How One Superintendent Improved School Community Relations*, The Administrator, July '97.
· *Minority Students Can Score Too*, The Educator, October '89.
· *How I Picked Up a School That Lost It's Leader in Mid Year*, National Association of Elementary School Principals,s May '85.

Brenda A. Bright

Certification:

· Continuing Superintendent Certificate, Gonzaga University	1999
· Continuing Principal Certificate, Washington State University	1989
· Continuing Teacher Certificate, Washington State University	1981

Civic Activities:

· Secretary, League of Women Voters, Medical River, Washington.
· Member, Medical River Chamber of Commerce.
· Treasurer, Assembly of God Church, Spokane, Washington.
· Vice President, Lions Club of Prairie Heights.
· Vice President, Richville Chamber of Commerce.
· President, Richville Youth Soccer Association.

Professional Organizations:

· Member, American Association of School Administrators.
· Member, Washington Association of School Administrators.
· Member, National Association of Secondary School Principals.
· Member, National Association of Elementary School Principals.
· Vice President, Washington Association of Elementary School Principals.
· President, Richville Education Association.

References:

Mrs. Joan Frost, Vice President, Medical River School Board of Directors	(509) 555–1715
E-mail,jfrost@medicalr.ed	
Mr. Jack B. Qwik, President, Medical River Education Association	(509) 555–2468
E-mail,jquik@medicalr.ed	
Chief of Police Jack Lawe, Medical River, Washington	(509) 555–9111
E-mail,jlaw@medicalr.pol	

Important Points

1. Your résumé should be individualized and demonstrate your strengths as they relate to the district's challenges and qualifications.
2. There is no absolute in the order of general categories. Place them in the order that best shows your strengths.
3. Emphasize results as much as possible in your résumé.
4. Have a colleague or mentor review the résumé. Then massage it to perfection.

Now you are an expert résumé writer. What is the best résumé? It is the one that will get you the interview. All that is left is to "wrap it up" with the rest of your application packet and "cast your net into the waters."

Paper clip the résumé pages together and put your papers in the following order: cover letter, application form, and résumé. Clip them together with a large paper clip, and place them in a 9x12 envelope. Address the envelope to the person you wrote the cover letter to and drop it in the mail. Or better yet, send it registered mail. That way, you are sure it will reach its destination.

You don't just sit back and wait for the phone calls, though. There is a lot more work to be done.

Chapter Six

Are You Ready For The Interview?

You have not received the call for the interview, but assume the call will come. Like a substitute in a football game, when the coach calls your number, be ready to play.

There is a protocol for job hunting for school administrators, but unlike other businesses, follow-up telephone calls to the school district office, school board members, or search consultants are frowned upon. All your questions should have been answered before you mailed your application packet.

Poor preparation means poor performance. You should use this time to prepare *your response to the phone call* and for the *interview* itself.

In Chapter One, I stated that the process for hiring differs in each school district. You will be interviewed by: a human resources person, assistant superintendent, a committee of citizens and staff, and the superintendent. Or a search consultant, parent/staff committee, and the school board, or a combination of all will interview you. My point is that you should have found out the process prior to applying for the job.

Each time I interviewed, I thought I had seen everything—but I haven't. A friend told me that he applied for a job as a principal of a large high school. An interview with an assistant superintendent narrowed the field to five. A staff/parent/student committee interviewed the finalists during the lunch period. The students observed the interviews on closed circuit television. The school board and superintendent interviewed the final three candidates.

More school districts are turning toward group interviews where all the finalists are in the same room, at the same time, with very large interview teams. They want to compare the candidates, side-by-side, and see how they react under extremely stressful conditions. Don't be intimidated by the crowd or the other candidates.

Additionally, districts send applicants to an assessment center prior to the interviews. Candidates are asked to do everything from analyzing a teacher lesson, and conducting mock evaluations. Some districts require candidates to take personality tests. I don't know if there are any sure-fire solutions to personality tests.

Many of the hiring districts send administrators and/or school board members on site visits of candidate's home districts. They are usually scheduled, but some are unannounced. You should anticipate such a visit.

Do your homework and be prepared for any eventuality. Most of the time the same questions or slightly different questions are asked. Try to find out as much as possible about the people that will be interviewing you. I am not suggesting that you change the answers to the questions, but changing the emphasis might be helpful. More about this later.

Find out about the school and school district

Stop by the school district office and request a brochure about the school and district. Check with the business office and get a copy of the current budget. Talk to colleagues in neighboring school districts about the reputation of the school and school system. Visit the local newspaper and read back issues. Be sure to read the editorial pages. That is where people provide their opinions.

Go to the local supermarket and ask about ten or twenty people what they think of the school and district. You will gain important information for the interview. Just as importantly, you indicate to people that you are interested in their school, district and community. Word gets around fast—especially in the smaller communities.

I have been told twice after I was hired that I was the only candidate that visited the district and community prior to the interview. I impressed them with my interest.

On another occasion a colleague had earlier worked in a district where I had applied for the superintendent vacancy. I called him and picked his brain about the district and community. My next to last question was, "Can you tell me the name of a community member that has lived there a number of years that can give me information about the community?" After he answered in the affirmative, my last question was, "What do you think would be the best approach I can use to meet him?"

He answered, "He's in the phone book. Call him and tell him that I suggested you talk with him. Offer to buy him lunch."

I called the gentleman that same day. He happened to have lived in the community most of his life. He was the editor of the newspaper, and one of the biggest school supporters in the area.

I met him for lunch, we spent three hours visiting, and it turned out that he had tremendous influence with the school board. I must have passed his "informal" interview because he not only supported me when I interviewed for the job, but also for the seven years that I was superintendent.

I don't recommend contacting the current principal or superintendent. You don't know the real reason that they are transferring or retiring. If they are departing on a negative note you don't want them supporting you.

Interview questions

Only so many different questions can be asked—and they are usually similar. It has been my experience that there are some questions or statements that are always part of the interview (This is not really a question, but a statement):

"Please take a few minutes to tell us about yourself."

This is the way an interview usually starts. This is your opportunity to make a positive first impression. Remember the old saying, "You don't have a second chance to make a good first impression." Most candidates answer this with a chronological listing of their birth, schools and work experiences. *Don't.* This is your chance to get the interviewer(s) on your side. Enthusiastically recount your life story with comments that will help you be likable and so the interviewer(s) can relate to you. Intertwine your experiences with the *challenges and qualifications* in the vacancy announcement brochure. Remember that they are looking for a person that has those qualifications. For example, "At Old Hat U. I met Professor Smith. He taught me the importance of collaborative leadership." "While principal at New School High, I gained appreciation for the importance of good school community relations. If you get the interviewer(s) on your side in the first two minutes, regardless of your answers later, the person will side with you. This is a powerful fact about human nature. Understand it and use it to your advantage. They will always ask:

"Do you have any questions?"

The correct answer is "Yes." I like to have at least five "knock out" questions that are designed to make a favorable impression with the interviewers. None of them are "What is the salary?" After I had landed a job as superintendent, one of the board members told me that another member went into the interview with a "lukewarm" feeling about me. My research revealed that he was interested in computers in the schools. She said that when I asked the school board, "What is your commitment to technology in the schools?" She thought the hesitant school board member was going to leap across the table and kiss me.

Many times the interviewers will close the interview by asking you if you have any other comments or would you like to say something that did not fit into the interview questions. You should respond by summarizing your qualifications as relates to the *challenges and qualifications* in the vacancy brochure. Close by saying words to the effect:

"Now that I have met and visited with you, I am
even more interested in the position. Thank you for
the interview. I am pleased to have met you."

Some questions and sample answers

What qualifications do you have that make you think you are a good fit for this position?

There is no correct response except your answer should relate your experience with the challenges and qualifications in the vacancy brochure.

Why are you leaving your current position?

Many people make the mistake of answering that they are perfectly happy where they are, but they have been waiting for this vacancy and this is the only job they will pursue. Does that sound too maudlin to you? It will to other people as well.

Suggest: A sincere comment that you are looking to advance yourself. If there are special circumstances, do not be afraid to mention them— unless it is for a divorce. Employers prefer their leaders to have a stable home life. They want leaders to solve problems, not bring new ones.

Does your current employer know you are looking for a job?

Suggest: My present boss is aware that I am looking for more of a challenge. I have not informed the district that I am leaving.

What is your major weakness?

Don't say you don't have one—everyone has at least one. Besides, it is important for you to know your shortcomings so that you can work to improve.

Suggest: I have a difficult time recognizing that not everyone is as dedicated to kids and schools as I am. I used to lose patience with them, but now I recognize that other people's priorities are different, and I am improving.

What are your three greatest strengths?

You recognize that you have many, but you must realize that the interviewer is only asking for three. Hence, you must prioritize.

Suggest: I would say my loyalty, people skills and dedication to the job.

Why are you a good leader?

Site several accomplishments that you have had.

Suggest: I recognize that the key to success is hiring good employees. I have a keen eye for hiring the best. Then I step back and allow them to do their job. We worked together to reorganize the curriculum, and our test scores improved considerably.

What have you liked least about previous jobs and employers?

*This is a no-brainer. **Never, never, never** say negative things about previous bosses or districts.*

Suggest: I have worked with people and in buildings those were challenges. I believe that I am a problem solver, so I look forward to new challenges.

What have you done in your life or career that you are most proud?

Be especially excited and enthusiastic as you respond to this question. Cite a couple of your awards, but bring it back to kids.

Suggest: When Wishwash Chamber of Commerce selected me Man of the Year, I was really pleased. When I was nominated Principal of the Year nationwide, I was especially gratified. There have been so many proud moments. But I think the proudest I am is every year when I go to high school commencement exercises and see the happy graduates and know I had a small part in their success.

What were the characteristics of your best bosses?

Be brief with your answer. This one has land mines all around it.

Suggest: My present boss best characteristic is her excellent communication skills. She is very knowledgeable, and always willing to help me. She has been a wonderful mentor. I have never had a supervisor for whom I did not respect. Each person has been different and I have been able to learn from his or her strengths and weaknesses.

Why have you moved around to so many districts so often?

If you have moved around a lot in the past, she may not think you plan to remain in her district. You want to convince her that there were logical reasons for your move, but you would like to remain here longer.

Suggest: I have moved progressively to larger schools as principal. I have spent the last three years at Lonely Hill and really like being superintendent of the district, but it is small. It seems there is always a mountain of paper work with no help. This district is larger and I will have help with paper work so I can get out and communicate with staff, parents and kids.

There are invariably other questions that may appear during the interviews—especially some peculiar to each specific job. Other questions are pretty generic. Most of the questions or slight changes to the questions will be part of the interview. You get the idea now? I have listed some sample questions at Appendix A.

Preparing the questions and answers for the interview

- Sit down at your computer and list all of the questions appropriate to the position for which you are applying.
- Write the answers that you expect to give the interviewer.
- Be sure to include the first question and answer about your background, and your summary statement, which will conclude the interview.
- Massage your responses so that they sound like you talking.
- Read both the question and answer onto a cassette tape.
- Play the tape several times each day. The tape deck in the car on the way to and from work is always a good time. You don't want to commit the answers to memory. You just want to be completely familiar with them. When the questions are asked during the interview, you only have to think about how you are going to phrase your response. After several days of listening, have a spouse or friend sit down at a table with you and role play, asking the questions while you provide the answers. Do this several times, practicing enthusiasm, voice inflection and body language. These practice sessions will be refined in a later chapter.

Important Points

1. Use the time between the submission of your application packet and telephone call to prepare yourself for the interview.
2. Procedures differ in all the school districts.
3. You may be interviewed by: A search consultant; central office staff member, a committee of staff, community members and students; school board; or superintendent. Or you may be interviewed by two or more—not in any particular order.
4. Visit the school and district to find out as much as possible about them.
5. Talk with colleagues about the school and district.
6. Try to meet with a civic leader to get information about the school and district.
7. Prepare your opening statement so that it is not only a chronological review of your life, but also relate experiences with the district brochure's challenges and qualifications.
8. Prepare five "knock out" questions. Have them in writing, and during the interview, pick two of the most appropriate questions to ask.
9. Have a summary statement prepared in advance so that you can enthusiastically re-count your strengths. End it with a phrase complimenting the district and indicating further interest in the job.
10. Choose the appropriate questions from the list at Appendix A. Write your response to each of them.
11. Put the questions and your response on a tape recorder and play the tape several times so that you have them committed to memory.
12. Rehearse the interview with your spouse or friend. Emphasize enthusiasm, voice inflection, and body language.

Chapter Seven

Will You Get the Telephone Call for an Interview?

In the next three chapters, we will use Dr. Brenda Bright as an example. We will follow her through the process.

Bright is at home listening to the tape of her interview questions and answers when the phone rings. She rushes to it, takes a deep breath, lets it out slowly and says, "Hello."

"Hello, is this Dr. Brenda Bright?"

"Yes it is. What can I do for you?"

"This is Mrs. Josephine Shmuck, consultant for the job search for the superintendent vacancy at Cripple Creek School District. I wonder if you are available to sit down and talk with me in the next few days?"

In a couple short seconds Bright screams, "All-right!" to herself, takes another deep breath and collects her thoughts. She knows she has an interview, so she needs to follow her plan.

This phone call may come from a consultant, director of the district Human Resources department, or an assistant superintendent. You should have a list of questions on your person to help you separate yourself from the pack. The remainder of the conversation should go something like this:

"Yes, Mrs. Shmuck. You say you represent Cripple Creek School District?" (Bright is implying that she has applications elsewhere).

"Yes. You are one of eight candidates that my screening committee has given me to interview. Are you available in the next few days?"

"I'll be happy to meet with you. What time and which day are you starting the interviews?" (You want to try to be the first one interviewed to set the standard for the rest, or the last one interviewed to leave the last impression).

"The interviews will begin promptly at 9:00 AM on Wednesday."

"That works fine for me because I have some important meetings this week. Where may I meet you at 9:00 AM on Wednesday? (It seems Bright was the first candidate Shmuck called, so she has the chance to be the first one interviewed–good).

"I have a temporary office above the post office in Cripple Creek. Do you know where it is located?"

"I'll be there Wednesday at 9:00 AM. I have a few questions, do you have the time now to discuss them?"

"Sure, how can I help you?"

"What is the process and time line for the interviews?"

"Well, you will not have to bring anything to your interview with me. It will just be you and me and we will primarily discuss your application packet. When we meet I will have a written time line."

"That's fine, can you just give me a review of the time line now?"

"Of course. I will interview all eight candidates by close of business Friday. I will meet with the board on Sunday and give them my report. The board will interview the five semi-finalists all day Tuesday. Someone will call the three finalists Wednesday night. Each of them will spend a day in the district meeting staff. They will have dinner with the board and meet the community at 8:00 PM. That will take place on Wednesday, Thursday, and Friday. Board members will make a visit to the finalists' home districts on Monday, The board will then meet on Wednesday, compare notes and make their decision. They will meet the winning candidate on Friday to discuss the contract."

"Will there be a writing exercise?" (You want to know this in advance so that if there is, you can ask if a computer is available. If no computer is accessible, you can ask if you can bring your laptop).

"Yes there is a one page writing exercise. A computer will be available."

"That's fine. Will anyone else besides the board be at the second interview?"

"Just the board. The board secretary will take each candidate through the written exercise after each interview."

"I think you have answered all my questions. I look forward to meeting you on Wednesday, Mrs. Shmuck. Good-bye."

Bright hangs up the phone and her mind races a mile a minute. So much to do and so little time. This is Friday. and she has less than five days to prepare for two interviews. The interviews are completely different. Bright decides to plan for a desk side interview with Shmuck and a very formal "interrogation" interview with the board a week later.

Rehearse

Even though Shmuck told Bright that she would merely review her packet, Bright is unsure what that really means. Bright will simply clarify parts of the contents of her packet, or Shmuck will ask her follow-up questions to statements on the résumé.

She might say, "I notice that you improved the cash carryover to five percent. How did you accomplish that?" Or she might say, "Tell me about your K–12 cultural diversity curriculum."

Bright takes the district's vacancy brochure and reviews *the challenges and qualifications,* her cover letter and résumé. She looks where she gave examples of actions that she took that related to the *challenges and qualifications.* Shmuck went to a great deal of trouble putting together the *challenges and qualifications* for the school board. She wants to be sure that she delivers five people that meet the *challenges and qualifications.*

Bright typed the examples on her computer and typed in follow-up responses. Then she put the information on a tape and listened to it several times a day Saturday and Sunday.

On Monday and Tuesday, she set up a table with a chair on each side. She had her spouse play the role of Mrs. Shmuck, and practiced the interview. Bright practiced the greeting, the interview and the farewell. She practiced enthusiasm, voice inflection, eye contact and body language. Bright videotaped the interview and played it back. She worked to eliminate the "ahs," "ummms" and "you knows." She also looked for and eliminated the following negative body language:

· Folding her arms across her chest.
· Leaning back and slumping in her chair.
· Putting her hand(s) to her face—especially her mouth.
· Playing with her hair.
· Glancing at her watch or a clock in the room.
· Excessive hand gestures.

Bright checked her posture, facial expressions and voice tone and inflection. She wanted to:

· Sit up straight in the chair and lean slightly forward, or toward the interviewer.
· Maintain eye contact.
· Smile, but not excessively.
· Laugh when appropriate, but don't try to be a humorist.
· Display confidence and enthusiasm, both in body language and voice tone and inflection.

A former administrator had several interviews and could not land a job. I told him that his strength as an administrator worked against him in an interview. He had a laid back demeanor and low voice that defused conflicts when dealing with students and parents. He took the same demeanor and voice to interviews and gained no ground. I worked with him for two hours on interview techniques. He landed a job after the next interview.

Nothing can help you get a job if you just try to "wing it." Practice, practice, practice. Interviewing is a learned skill, not an inherent quality. Your answers to questions, although memorized, will eventually come off as unrehearsed.

Find out as much as you can about the background of the consultant. It is fairly easy to find out about in-state consultants, but almost impossible to find background about national search consultants. Does she have a background as a school administrator? If so, where? Where was she born? Where did she go to school? You are looking for some common ground. You are looking for a connection.

These queries should be very discreet because they could backfire on you. You don't want the consultant to know that you are making inquiries, no matter how innocent. Your goal is to come out of the interview with the consultant thinking, "I really like that person."

Dirty tricks

I have not heard of a search consultant for education administrators doing this. However, I have heard of some businesses doing it when hiring executives. They want to see how the interviewee reacts to stress. They manufacture some stress:

- If you find yourself waiting 30–60 minutes past the appointment time, the consultant wants to see how you react.
- Another way is to have you looking out a window with the consultant sitting in front of the window and the bright sun coming in from her back. The pupils of your eyes contract, letting less light in. Your interviewer appears as a shadow, and you cannot see her expression, eyes or body language. Not to mention that it causes fatigue.
- Finally, she may throw in a controversial subject to see how you react. The important thing to do is prepare yourself for this to happen. When it occurs, just figure it is all part of the process and do not be upset by it.

To do checklist

✔ Review the brochure and write questions and answers.
✔ Put answers on tape and listen to them for three days.
✔ Rehearse the interview for two days prior to the interview.

✔ Take your suit/dress and shirt/blouse to the cleaners/laundry.
✔ Get a fresh hair cut or get your hair done.
✔ Be sure you have a pair of shoes that are comfortable and are not in disrepair.
✔ Figure out what time you have to get up to have time to:
  ☐ Eat breakfast.
  ☐ Clean and polish shoes.
  ☐ Take a bath or shower.
  ☐ Shave/brush teeth/do hair, etc.
  ☐ Clean and clip fingernails.
✔ Figure out what time you have to leave home or the motel to arrive in town at least forty-five minutes before the appointment. (Remember to have your tape in the car so that you can listen to it on the way to the appointment. If you concentrate on the tape you do not fill your head with negative thoughts about the interview).

Dress

Make no mistake—clothing makes the administrator. Don't let anyone tell you otherwise. I could take you through a long litany of colors that say you are optimistic, good-natured, affectionate, sophisticated, etc. But if you wore all those colors, you would look like a rainbow. People don't want their administrators to resemble a rainbow.

You want people to have confidence in you. Dress for success—even if you are interviewing for your first administrator job.

Employees don't wear business suits in some businesses, and even some school districts. Don't be fooled if you visit the district in advance and see everyone in the central office wearing casual clothing. People hold principals and superintendents to a higher standard. You can always "dress down" after you have won the job.

I learned during my military career that people act the way that they are dressed. You want to exude confidence and high self-esteem. The business suit will help you "feel" confident.

Remember that your appearance is part of the all-important first impression. I recommend a navy or black business suit for men and the same color business suit or dress for women. If you do not have one, it is a wonderful investment for your future. Pick out a suit or dress that is a good fit and is not thread worn.

Men wear a white shirt, with a red, blue striped, or maroon necktie. I like to wear a tie that is navy blue, with red and white stripes—for obvious reasons. Have the shirt freshly laundered with some starch. Send the suit and tie to the cleaners. Women wear a white or cream blouse with the suit. Both should be freshly dry cleaned.

Men, wear a pair of black shoes that do not have worn soles or heals. Clean and polish them the day before and the day of the interview. Wear over-the-calf black sox. The only jewelry worn should be a wristwatch and one ring.

Women wear matching low to medium (1–2 inch) heeled shoes, with dark panty hose (Yes, even if it is 100 degrees in the shade). Wear small earrings, a watch and one ring, and carry a small purse or briefcase.

Important Points

1. Be prepared with written questions before the consultant telephones you.
2. Find out from the consultant:
   - How the initial interview fits in with the search process.
   - Are other interviews planned?
   - If other interviews are planned, by whom?
   - Are the identities of the candidates still confidential?
   - Are site visits planned?
   - What is the timetable for the activities?
3. Try to be either the first or last candidate to be interviewed.
4. Plan two interviews, but rehearse only the initial interview now.
5. Use a video camera for the rehearsals to help eliminate flaws, such as negative body language, posture, eye contact, voice inflection, and improve your confidence.
6. Find out as much about the consultant as you can. You are trying to form a bond between the two of you.

7. Be prepared for "dirty tricks" during the interview. Do not let them bother you.
8. Prepare a list of tasks to be accomplished prior to the interview.
9. Plan the attire you will wear to the interview and get it dry-cleaned.
10. Take care of personal grooming.

Dr. Bright carefully planned the next five days. A reminder that getting a job is hard work. Don't take anything for granted. Your preparation will show in an excellent interview.

Chapter Eight

The Interviews

As I stated in earlier chapters, the interview may be in several different forms. It may be with a consultant; a human resources person; an interview committee composed of community members, staff, and students; the school board; or the superintendent. Further, the interviews may be in different orders, depending on the location and the position vacancy.

We will discuss an interview by a consultant, by school board, and by a community forum. The procedures for interviews by the human resources person and the superintendent are generally the same. The process for the school board and a committee of parents, staff, and students are very similar.

A few general comments:
· Remember that once the interview process has begun, you are always being observed. If you take the wrong step, it will get back to the decision maker(s). Don't lower your guard—no matter how tempting.
· If it is a daylong process, bring along extra clothing or a shirt/blouse—especially if it involves an evening dinner or a public forum.
· Treat everyone with respect and politeness.

The interview with the consultant

It is the night before the interview. Dr. Bright finished her rehearsals and felt that she was ready. A good night's sleep is very important. Interviews are stressful, and you will need all the energy you can muster. If you have to get up a little earlier to drive to the interview site, then go to bed earlier.

Once you arise, take a quick bath and wash and dry your hair. Believe it or not—interviewers look closely at your hair. Use a strong, non-aromatic deodorant. You will perspire during the interview, and you will need all the help you can get. Check your hands to be sure they are clean and your fingernails clipped and clean.

A word about facial hair: there are two schools of thought about male facial hair. Some people like facial hair; others do not. Some folks think a beard shows trust. Others do not trust someone with a mustache. My advice is–if possible, eliminate facial hair *unless* a complete shave affects your psyche to the point that it would be detrimental to your interview performance. It is a decision only you can make. Women should remove facial hair and shave their legs.

If possible, dress in casual clothes when the drive to the interview site exceeds one hour. Carry your interview clothes in a garment bag and find a rest room near the site to change so there is less chance of your interview "uniform" becoming spotted or wrinkled.

If you have followed my recommendations, you have already driven to the interview site. Remember that you went there to talk to staff and community members to find out something about the district. You should have already figured out where to go to change clothes.

Odor is also an important consideration. Men should use a subdued after shave lotion and women a very mild perfume. Some people are allergic to strong cologne and perfume. You do not want to be the one that runs into the allergic interviewer. Moreover, the interviews are usually conducted in a small conference room and last more than an hour.

If you smoke, don't do so once you have bathed. Take a breath mint before entering the reception area, and do not accept coffee if offered. *Coffee breath* is a real turn-off to some people. Strong aromas of any kind can turn people off to your other skills.

Check your pocket or purse to be sure you have your "knock out" questions to ask. Be sure the list is easily accessible.

Arrive at the interview site at least fifteen minutes early, sit in the parking lot, and study your interview questions. Don't report to the receptionist until five minutes before the appointed time. Promptness is important, but if you arrive too early, you may disrupt the interviewer, and she may feel pressured. Just be on time. I can not tell you how many college graduates lost a chance for a job before the interview even started because they did not show up on time. Many consultants and interviewers have their receptionist jot down the time the candidate reported to her.

When you report to the receptionist, use a friendly smile and say, "Good morning, I'm Brenda Bright and I have an interview appointment at 9:00 with Mrs. Shmuck." Don't try to make small talk with the receptionist. She has other duties to perform. She will probably have candidates sitting near her desk most of the day.

When Mrs. Shmuck greets you, make sure she extends her hand first. Some people do not like to shake hands. Keep your hand by your side until she extends her hand forward. A nice firm handshake is important. *Women:* a wet, wash rag, handshake is a thing of the past. *Men:* don't try to break bones in her hand to show your manliness. Practice on a spouse or a female friend until you get the right amount of pressure.

Your initial greeting might go something like this, "Hi, Mrs. Shmuck, I'm Brenda Bright. It's a pleasure to meet you." A warm, friendly smile should remain on your face as you maintain eye contact. When asked to be seated, do not move the chair. She has it in that spot for a reason. Don't get too comfortable. Make some flattering small talk, such as, "What a nice office you have." Or if it isn't a nice office, say, "Your directions to your office were perfect. Thank you." Or, "Thank you for the information you gave me on the telephone. It's nice to meet you." Then be *quiet.* Remember it is *her* interview.

Look around at the room, desk area, and the interviewer. There are clues everywhere that can help you leave a good impression. These clues tell you about the interviewer's personality and how you can deal with her. There are four basic personalities:

Congenials: outgoing, energetic, friendly, and self-assured. Look for the following clues:

· Flamboyant and fashionable style of dress. Even in a suit they wear a bright colored tie or scarf. They usually wear flashy accessories.
· There are numerous pictures and trappings in the office.
· The desk is cluttered and covered with work.
· They are not conscious of time, so you may be kept waiting. He or she is trying to do several things at once. They have to like you before they will listen to you. Listening is not on their list. You will need to smile more, talk faster, and get to the point. If you are also this type, a word of caution. You do not want to out-talk, out-smile or out-interview the interviewer.

Honchos: better known as "Master." These people differ from Congenials because they are far more reserved. Clues to look for are:

· Conservative, high-quality, custom-tailored clothing.
· A neat and organized office. A few expensive personal desk accessories. One or two fancy picture frames containing family photos. Everything is understated.
· A firm handshake, but not a smiler. Not nearly as talkative as the Congenial. They will size you up and wait for you to make a mistake.
· They are time conscious and goal oriented and annoyed when others are not.

You must be all business with this type. Don't waste the interviewer's time. Be sincere and eliminate unnecessary words. He or she does not like being around "touchy-feely" people. Don't be intimidated. If you are, Honchos will sense it and reject you immediately.

Scholars: analytical types. They don't socialize, speak up, or editorialize. They get their work done properly by going about their business quietly. Clues to look for:

· Gray and beige, drab clothes. Style and looks are not a priority. This is a pragmatic individual.
· Few personal items and "warm fuzzies" in their work space. An organized desk with work neatly arranged. Might even have a to-do list with some of the items crossed off.
· This interviewer will have a limp handshake. Shake it anyway. It will confirm your suspicions that he or she is a Scholar.
· Their work ethic is just as strong as the Honchos. They are loners that are time conscious and work oriented.

This person may be difficult to draw out and may become angry if you try. They thrive on data but need time to analyze it. Answer questions directly and succinctly. Volunteer only as much information as you think the interviewer needs.

Allies: non-aggressive Congenials. These are usually the Human Resources Director types because they will go to great ends not to make a decision. Clues to look for are:

- Neutral shades and soft fabrics that are nonthreatening.
- Their office will reflect that people are important to them. Look for personal items on their desk—many of them handmade.
- They are friendly, expressive, and concerned. They may apologize profusely for keeping you waiting—because they were busy solving other people's problems.
- To an Ally, people are all that matters. These are the opposite of Honchos. The Ally helps but does not hire. Take time to establish rapport. It is your job to get your job qualifications across in the interview. Become friends and accentuate the importance of "personal in personnel."

Some interviewers will fit the stereotypes to a tee. Others will fit into several of the categories. You may see personality classifications with different names, but they are close to those mentioned. Study the four types and practice typecasting a few of your friends and relatives. Learn to pick up on the clues of someone's dominant personality type, then practice playing to them. Take the time to do this. It is another way of helping you finish a cut above the rest.

During the interview

Keep in mind that the subject of the interview is *you*. And *you* know more about *you* then the interviewer does. Keep that in mind as you try to eliminate your nervousness. Maintain a positive attitude throughout the interview—even if you think the interview is going badly.

Try to "mirror" the interviewer's body language, facial expressions, eye movement, tone of voice, and rate of speech. This is a subtle art that requires practice, or you may come across as "mimicking" her.

This subtle form of imitation is a proven way to establish rapport. It is a basic form of physical agreement.

Be a student of body language. If you notice the interviewer is sitting up straight, fidgeting, folding her arms, or looking away when you are talking, take the hint. Either stop talking or change the subject. If you are not doing well at what you are doing, do not compound the problem by continuing. If you can read the body language, be smart enough to make the necessary adjustments. You may still be able to convince her.

Pay attention to *eye signals* both in the interviewer and yourself. If a listener looks away from the speaker, it may indicate that she is not satisfied or disagrees with what has been said. It could also mean she is trying to conceal her reaction to the speaker's words. If you look away when you are speaking, you are not certain of what you are saying.

The important thing to keep in mind is that you must persuade the interviewer to come away from the meeting with intuitive positive feelings about you. She may not be able to explain specifically why, but she will have developed them nonetheless.

Conclusion of the interview

The last question the interviewer will usually ask will be, "Do you have any questions?" Your response should be, "Yes I do. I have them written down." Remove them from your purse or briefcase, scan them, and pick out the two you believe to be the most appropriate.

Don't ask questions that have already been answered during the interview. Pick out the two you think will help convince the interviewer you are the person for the job.

As you leave the office, thank her for the interview. Conclude the interview something like this: with a smile and an outstretched hand say, "Thank you for the interview, Mrs. Shmuck. I have enjoyed our discussion. I hope to hear from you in the near future." Shake her hand firmly but gently. On the way out, stop and thank the receptionist.

Do you relax and rest? No. Go to your car in the parking lot and jot down notes about the interview that will help you at the next interview.

Have a thank you note already addressed to Shmuck. Make it hand-written, short, and sweet. Say something like, "Thank you for the interview. It was a pleasure meeting with you. Good luck during the rest of the search." Drop it in the mail the same day.

You have more rehearsals—even though you do not know if there will be another interview. Maintain your positive attitude and begin preparing for the interview with the school board.

Keep in mind the following recent research from *How To Land The Best Jobs In School Administration,* by Georgia Kosmoski, about interview committees:

Who hires male candidates?

One that is composed of mostly administrators.
One that is composed of mostly males.
One that is small to average in size.

Who hires female candidates?

One that is composed mostly of teachers.
One that is composed mostly of females.
One that is average to large in size.

Basically, Bright must prepare for the next interview as she did for Shmuck, except that she must multiply one person times however many school board members are present. For this illustration, let's assume five members will conduct the interview.

Dr. Bright is following my step-by-step method of cutting herself out of the pack and has done her homework about the board members' backgrounds. She found one is the stay at home spouse of an engineer and very active in community activities. Another is a building contractor that is a computer whiz. Another is a retired roads commissioner who believes strongly in reading, writing, and arithmetic. A fourth is a social worker for the state. The last is the spouse of a former school administrator. This knowledge will help her—as long as she uses it during the interview.

Bright decides to ask the board the following questions:

- What is the district's commitment to technology in the schools?
- From our discussion, I understand that you want the district to stay on the cutting edge of curriculum and teaching. Do you expect basics to suffer—i.e., readen, ritin and rithmetic?
- Does the district work closely with local authorities such as child welfare services?
- How committed is the district to having businesses and community members active in the schools?
- How do you see the duties of the school board in relation to the responsibilities of the superintendent in managing the district? (You would ask each member to respond.)

Bright figures she will not have to memorize any more questions and answers—they will probably be the same as for the Shmuck interview. Since Bright is interviewing for the superintendent job, if hired she will work directly for the school board. Therefore, she should place emphasis on the following:

- Connect with *all* of them.
- They are looking for someone that thinks like them and communicates with them.
- They are looking for someone that is "kid oriented."
- They are looking for someone that can make tough decisions.
- They are looking for someone that fits the profile outlined in the *challenges and qualifications* brochure.

Dr. Bright had her spouse help her practice. She remembered to videotape the interview, noting her body language, verbal responses, and eye contact. Bright made corrections each time until she was perfect.

Your posture is the same, except that regardless of who asks the question, you respond orally and sweep the entire room, back-and-forth, making eye contact with every board member. You are trying to connect with all five of them. If you ignore or snub one of them, it might just happen to be the *informal* leader who can convince the other four members another candidate is better.

On Sunday, Dr. Bright waits nervously by the telephone. At 8:00 PM, and about the time she thought she would not be called, the telephone rang. She held her breath as she answered it.

"Hello, Dr. Bright, this is Mrs. Shmuck. Good news. You are one of the five candidates the board will interview on Wednesday."

"Well, that is wonderful news, Mrs. Shmuck. I was beginning to think I was not going to get a call."

"Oh, no. The board meeting just ended, and you are the first one on the list for me to call. I was pleased with our talk on Wednesday."

"Well, thank you. I enjoyed our meeting, too. Can I expect to be interviewed at 9:00 AM again on Tuesday?" (Remember that you want to be either the first or last person interviewed.)

"Yes. The interview will be in the boardroom at the school district office. Do you know where it is located?"

"That's great. Yes. I visited the district office a couple weeks ago to pick up a school descriptive guide and budget."

"Well, that's fine. I still have some more calls to make. If you have any other questions, please do not hesitate to call me."

Dr. Bright hangs up the phone and her mind is racing. She tells herself to relax and go back to her checklist from the previous interview. The first thing she has to do is get her interview "uniform" back to the cleaners.

It is Tuesday morning, and Dr. Bright just pulled into the parking lot of the district office. She meets the receptionist with a smile the same way she did at the Shmuck interview.

After waiting about five minutes, a gentleman enters, offers his hand, and says, "Hi, You must be Dr. Bright. I'm Don Smith, the board president. Welcome to Cripple Creek School District."

Bright shakes his hand firmly but gently, smiles, and says, "Good morning Mr. Smith. Thank you. I appreciate the invitation and welcome." (You never get familiar. Even if they address you by your first name, you always address them formally with Mr., Mrs., or Ms.)

Smith ushers Bright into a room that looks to be about 16'x16'square with a large round table in the center. A coffeepot, juice container, and water pitcher are on a table near a wall. Two men and two women are seated at the table.

There are two empty chairs nearest the door. The four people all stand up as Smith and Bright enter the room. Smith walks to the table, stands near an empty chair, gestures toward the last empty chair, smiles, and says, "This is your chair, the hot seat."

Everyone laughs together, including Bright. She remembers not to be seated, yet. Bright smiles and reminds herself that she is to exude energy and enthusiasm.

She starts to her left and greets each board member, saying, "Good morning, I'm Brenda Bright."

They will probably put their right hand out to be shaken and respond with, "Hi, I'm Jane Doe, It's nice to meet you," or something like that.

Bright responds with another smile, shakes the outstretched hand, and repeats their name, "Pleased to meet you Ms. Doe."

She walks completely around the table introducing herself to each member individually, then takes her seat.

"Would you like, coffee, juice, or water?" Smith offers.

"Just a glass of water, please." You don't want that awful coffee smell on your breath, and juice may not agree with you. Water is necessary to clear your dry throat. Yes, it will get dry. It is also a great prop for that moment that you need extra time to think of an answer to a difficult question.

In a group interview, either the leader will ask all the questions, or the members will take turns asking questions. You have already rehearsed to be sure that even if only one of them asks the question, you direct your answer to all of them.

The members are cautioned not to ask follow up questions or get into dialogue because of time limitations, but the cautions are seldom followed. Don't concern yourself when they go off the script. It is the leader's responsibility to get them back on track. On one occasion, I was interviewed for four hours—and I got the job.

At the conclusion of the interview, Bright walks around the table, shakes hands again, and thanks every board member for the opportunity. The board president introduces Bright to the secretary, who leads her to an office with a computer.

I liked to have writing exercises when I was hiring because I felt it was important for an administrator to be able to communicate in writing. I know—you are thinking the cover letter and résumé should be a pretty good sample of writing ability. That may be true, but many people have them written or edited by someone else. If they are smart, they will at least have them edited by someone else.

The written exercise is usually a way to get you to write a thoughtful piece about a problem or about what you would do under a given set of circumstances. Take your time and give it careful thought. Outline your piece first. Compose the article, then go back and review it for content. Try to make it as simple as possible. Don't try to impress them with your large vocabulary. Use the computer's spell and grammar check. Make one last review, print it, and give it to the secretary. Be friendly and respectful with the secretary.

Once again, Dr. Bright goes to her car and jots down notes. You should always learn something that will help you in the next interview.

If the interview is with a group of seven to ten people and is composed of administrators, teachers, community members, parents, classified employees, and students, the same techniques apply. However, you should analyze your audience and try to connect with all of them. While they all share the importance of the brochure's *challenges and qualifications,* they have their own agenda. It bears repeating that the first impression is important, and you must give them all a sense that you connect with them—that you have something in common with each of them. You may want to change your opening statement if you can weave in stories about yourself that will connect you with the individuals.

Administrators are interested in your leadership style and problem solving techniques. Teachers and staff members will want assurances that you don't want to make wholesale changes and that you have a collaborative leadership style. Community members and parents are interested in your ability to communicate with the public and that you are child centered. Students are interested in your leadership style and that you are honest and fair. They are also looking for your "coolness."

About six months into a high school principalship, I was talking with the president of the student body. She happened to be the only student on the interview committee that hired me. I asked her what there was about me that convinced her that I was the person for the job. She replied, "Because you were the only one that talked directly to me. And you even asked me a question." Apparently the other candidates didn't see her as important in the selection process.

That evening the phone rings and Shmuck is on the phone.

"Hi, Brenda, its Josephine Shmuck again. It looks like you did real well during the interview. Congratulations."

Bright just can't hide her emotions this time. "Well, thank you. That is just terrific news," she gushes.

"As I told you, the next step is a long day. You are scheduled to have desk-side briefings all day and lunch with about twelve administrators. Dinner will be with the school board at 6:00 PM, and you meet with a community forum at 8:00 PM. I présumé that you want to be first again. Is that right?"

"Yes. I would like to go first. It sounds like a long day. Will I have time

to freshen up before dinner with the board?"

"Yes. Your day with the administrators ends at 4:00 PM. All right then, you will be at the district office at 9:00 AM tomorrow. The board secretary will give you a schedule. I probably will not see you again. Best of luck to you. Do you have any other questions?"

"Well, thank you. And thanks for all the help you have given me. Good-bye."

As Bright hangs up the phone, her mind seems to have slowed. The rest seems easy to her. But the next twenty-four hours is a test of stamina. They have her busy all day in district offices, give her just two hours to rest, then a stressful dinner, and finally a final test with the community.

Bright decides she is going to have to pace herself. She will have to be just as enthusiastic and full of energy in the evening as in the morning. "Make no mistake. You are on stage all day," Bright tells herself. She decides the community forum will be similar to the interview with the school board. Bright concludes that rest is more important than more rehearsals.

The administrators

They will be checking you out to see what your leadership style is and if changes will affect them. They will probably have a desk-side briefing prepared, telling you what they do and the resources they have to accomplish it. They will tell you their problems and try to get your reaction. If they do not have a briefing prepared, ask them for such a presentation. Ask them "neutral" questions. Don't tell them what you plan to do if hired—even if you have plans. Be friendly and enthusiastic. Convince all of them they have important jobs, and you will be depending on them if you are hired.

Always keep in mind that your job is to manage a district that is responsible for providing the best education possible for kids. Your responses should support that belief.

A few years ago, we were hiring a new high school principal. Part of the process was for the outgoing principal to take each candidate on a tour of the campus. He asked each candidate where he or she would like to start.

One candidate who did well on the interview replied, "Lets go to the gym."

After leaving the gym, he said, "Let's take a look at the football stadium."

They left the stadium and toured the classrooms and cafeteria area, and the outgoing principal said, "We have the music department and library left."

"That's OK, if you've seen one music department and library, you've seen them all."

The word got back to me, and I didn't hire that candidate. His actions indicated that he was interested in sports but not curriculum. Everything you do and say is under a microscope.

The meals

Advice for the meals is the same whether you are with administrators, board members, or anyone else. Review your table manners thoroughly. If you are not good at it, find a book and learn. As a school administrator, you are expected to attend many functions that include sit down meals.

Don't ask for or accept alcoholic beverages, even if others are imbibing. If you are expected to order from the menu, don't order the most expensive item. They will think you are a spendthrift. Don't order the cheapest because you might offend them. Do not offer to pay. You are their guest.

Since you will be questioned, don't expect to finish your meal. Besides, you don't want to eat a big meal. You want to be on your toes—not slowed down by overeating.

Order something that is light and easy to eat. You do not want to order spaghetti and have tomato sauce on you the rest of the day. Be careful about ordering a large salad because sometimes they are cumbersome and difficult to manage. I recommend a chicken breast or fish. They are usually in the middle of the menu in cost, are light to eat, manageable, and they are not "finger food."

Order an after dinner beverage, like tea, but *no* dessert. *Remember* that you want to keep alert. Demonstrate interest in the district, staff and board members by taking every opportunity to ask your hosts questions. Not just about the district but their personal lives. Besides, when they are answering your questions about themselves, they are not asking you questions. They are talking about their favorite subject—themselves. That is one of the ways you gain supporters—and at the same time, deflect questions away from you.

The community forum

This is usually held in the evening. Take the opportunity for a short rest and shower. Be sure to have a fresh set of clothes for the forum.

I have seen a situation where a moderator asks questions, and the candidate responds, then questions are asked from the floor. Other times, community members place questions in a box, and the moderator selects questions to ask.

You are primarily being tested on your ability to present yourself in front of a large group and think on your feet. Remember to analyze your audience. You will probably have staff, community members, board members, and even students in the audience. You want to connect with all of them. You want to exhibit friendliness, enthusiasm, and energy.

If you are asked to make an opening statement about yourself, use the time to give examples of your experiences that have prepared you to be able to meet *the challenges and qualification* listed in the brochure. You want to come across as friendly, accessible, a problem solver, kid-oriented, a supporter of staff, a collaborative leader, and be able to improve the district without making drastic changes.

They will ask you difficult questions, such as "How important do you think physical education is in the curriculum?" Or, "What are your feelings about extracurricular activities?" Or, "Tell us your thoughts about busing." There are probably some in the audience that disagree with you.

You need to make your responses as neutral as possible. For example you might answer the first question by saying, "If a child is physically fit, she stands a better chance of being alert and open to learning the basics."

Answer the second question with, "Academics are the single most important thing in the schools, but there is a place for extracurricular activities. Many kids do not share our enthusiasm for education. If we can entice them into the schools with extracurricular activities, we have a chance to teach them."

At the conclusion, thank the school board members for the opportunity to interview, the staff for their hospitality, and the community for their friendliness and openness. Compliment them on their kids, schools, and community. Tell them it would be an honor to work with them to improve the educational process of the Cripple Creek School District. Reassure them that you will be an active community member.

Important Points

1. Questions are usually the same whether interviewed by an individual, a committee, or at a public forum.
2. When being interviewed by an individual, you must try to make a connection or bond with her.
3. Recognize the four basic personalities in your interview and use them to your advantage.
4. When being interviewed by a group, you must concentrate on connecting with all of them—especially through eye contact.
5. If being interviewed by a school board, try to find out as much as possible about their backgrounds so you can connect with them better during the interview.

6. Do not get too familiar with interviewers. Always address them by their titles and last names.
7. Clothes and personal hygiene are important for an interview.
8. Remember school employees are concerned about how their lives may change. It is your job to allay those fears.
9. People expect administrators to be able to express themselves in writing. Be prepared to take a writing test.
10. You are being tested during a meal, so your table manners should be proper.
11. The minute you set foot in the school district, you are being tested. Don't lower your guard.
12. It is appropriate to send hand written thank you notes to interviewers.

Bright completed the day, went back to her motel room, closed the door, and sat on the chair near the bed. She leaned back and thought— this has been a great experience. I'm really glad I prepared myself in advance. The next hurdle is the site visit. That should be easy compared to this day. But this is no time for a mistake.

Chapter Nine

Closing the Deal

A word about thank you notes. I believe it is important that you send thank you notes after an interview. In other businesses, they recommend thank you or follow-up letters. I suggest a handwritten note on a thank you card. Mail it to all members of the committee or board the day they interview you.

The note should say, "Just a short note to thank you for the interview. It was a pleasure meeting with you today. You have a wonderful school or district. Even if I am not selected, I'm sure your school or district will continue to be one of the best in the state. Thanks again, and good luck!"

Very few candidates send thank you notes. The short-term effect is that if received in time, it may tip the scales to get you to the next interview or get you the job. The long-term effect is that it shows them you have class, and if another vacancy occurs, they will remember.

After I was interviewed by a school board for a job as high school principal, I sent each of them thank you notes. I didn't get the job. Years later, after I had become a superintendent, a school board member from that district approached me and struck up a conversation. Luckily, I remembered her from the previous interview.

She commented that I had been the only person she has ever seen to send a hand written thank you note. She commented that it was very classy. She informed me that an inside candidate had been hired for the principal job. Her district had a vacancy for superintendent, and she asked me if I would apply. I thanked her and told her that the timing was not convenient for a job switch.

The school board president called Dr. Bright on Saturday. He said he and another board member would visit her district on Monday at 9:00 AM.

By this time, the identity of the finalists has been made public. Even if you live in another state, either the consultant or Human Resources Director has contacted character references and other people in your home district. Word travels fast.

On Friday morning, Bright anticipated the call and had a meeting with her administrative staff to prepare them for the visit. She told them to be sure the buildings were clean and in good repair before Monday. She told them that they may or may not be visited. They were not to have any special briefings or presentations.

She picked her sharpest and most loyal administrator to wait in her office to guide them. Bright told her where to take them if she were given the choice.

At 9:00 AM sharp, Mr. Smith and Mrs. Doe arrived at the central office. Bright met them at the door and ushered them into her office where she had refreshments waiting.

After they each poured themselves a cup of coffee and took seats, Bright said, "I have cleared my calendar for the day and have made lunch reservations for us. However, I have Ms. Brown, my Public Relations Director available if you would rather have an escort other then me."

"We have arranged to fly home at 2:30 PM, so we will take you up on the lunch, then leave in time to catch our flight. We accept your kind offer to show us around your district," Smith answered.

Bright escorted them around the central office, the maintenance shop, and the bus garage—then one elementary, one junior high and one senior high building. They walked around and observed. They didn't enter any classrooms because they did not want to interrupt classes. Dr. Bright simply introduced the two as out-of-state visitors.

Fortunately, the number of students that greeted Dr. Bright and stopped to talk impressed the visitors.

The morning went fast and they went to a local restaurant for lunch. Several waitresses greeted Dr. Bright by name. (Naturally Bright picked the restaurant where she was best known. Bright wanted to show the visitors she got out in the community). Remembering she was still being interviewed, Dr. Bright chose a light fish meal.

Bright paid for the lunch with her credit card (vowing to make up the cost during contract negotiations). It would not be appropriate for her district to pay for the lunches of board members of a school district that is trying to hire her away. The visitors did not offer to pay for the lunch. Being new at this, they probably had not considered that they were still trying to woo a candidate.

On Wednesday evening, Bright was sitting at home watching her favorite television show when the phone rang.

"Hello, Dr. Bright, this is Mr. Smith, President of the Cripple Creek School District school board. How are you?"

Bright smiles as she talks, "Just fine. I hope you had a pleasant flight home?"

"Yes, we did. Thank you. The board has just finished a meeting. Are you still interested in coming to work with us?"

"If this is a contract offer, my answer is yes." She hears loud cheering in the background.

"As you can hear from my colleagues, we are all excited about you. Yes. It is a contract offer."

"I'm really excited about Cripple Creek School District, and I am looking forward to working with you and the rest of the board. What's next?"

"If you're available, we would like to schedule a Friday evening meeting to discuss your contract."

"That sounds fine. What time and where?"

"How about the school district board room at 7:00 PM?"

"Great. I am really looking forward to seeing you all again. Good-bye."

Contract negotiations are Bright's forte, and she has already started her preparation. When she visited the district office earlier, she introduced herself to the current superintendent and asked him for a copy of his contract. Further, she called the state School Administrators' Association and had a copy of an Annual Salary and Benefits Study for State School Administrators and a sample superintendent contract sent to her. A copy of a sample school superintendent contract is at Appendix B.

She needs to know what the current superintendent is being paid, and how it relates to other salaries in that area. She also needs to know what sort of benefits other administrators in that area are receiving. Armed with that important information, Bright makes up a list of questions.

Questions for negotiations
- ✔ Length of contract
- ✔ Renewal of employment contract
- ✔ Evaluation, goals, and objectives
- ✔ Salary
  - ☐ Gross annual salary
  - ☐ Cost of living increases
  - ☐ Merit increases (If so, when and what criteria are they based on)
- ✔ Insurance
  - ☐ Life insurance
  - ☐ Health, dental, eye
  - ☐ Cost per month
  - ☐ Deductible
  - ☐ If she elects not to take the insurance, what can be added to the package?
- ✔ Retirement
  - ☐ What is available?
  - ☐ Since Bright is from out of state, she must consider 401–K or some other

tax sheltered annuity as a retirement package, equal to someone on the state retirement plan.

✔ Vacation days
✔ Sick days
    ☐ Can unused sick or vacation days be sold back to the school district?
✔ Performance bonus.
✔ Personal protection and clause about firing
✔ Medical examination
✔ Professional growth time and funds
✔ Automobile needs for job
    ☐ Provide district car or car allowance
    ☐ If car allowance, how much
✔ Clause that superintendent has authority to move employees within the district
✔ Moving expenses
✔ Is consulting work allowed

Bright takes a copy of the current superintendent's contract to her professional association and meets with a contract advisor. The school board will probably expect her to sign a similar contract.

The advisor and Bright review the contract together and determine if it is what she wants. Three important clauses are in the contract:

· There must be cause for firing.
· The superintendent has the authority to transfer employees throughout the district.
· The superintendent can perform consulting as long as it does not interfere with her duties.

Dr. Bright compared the contracts and made a written list of what she needed in her contract. She recalls something her mentor told her years ago.

· You will never get another contract from a district as good as your first one, regardless of how long you remain there.
· A good rule of thumb is expect to be paid lower on the scale if this is your first principal or superintendent job. If you have had experience in the position for which you are negotiating a contract, expect to be paid at least as much as the outgoing leader.

School board members don't usually have experience in contract negotiations. Moreover, they are not familiar with negotiating salaries the size of a superintendent's. They invariably try to get the superintendent at the cheapest possible price.

When I negotiated a contract with a school board, they offered me a contract that was considerably different than the one given the former superintendent. I read it over carefully as they all sat quietly watching me.

I carefully placed the contract on the table, looked each of them in the eye, and said, "Why would you want to hire someone that would be stupid enough to sign a contract for only two thousand dollars more than the assistant superintendent?"

One of the board members laughed and said, "See there. I told you he wouldn't go for it."

Everyone laughed, and from that moment on our negotiations went fast, and I got most of what I wanted in the agreement. The language in the contract we arrived at was much different than I had anticipated. At the conclusion of the negotiations, I said, "Before signing the contract, I would like to take it to my professional organization and have it reviewed."

The board president said, "We had hoped to be able to approve your hire tonight, but we understand. When can we meet again?"

"I believe I can have it reviewed in a day and be back day after tomorrow."

"I'm really concerned. Can't you just sign something now?" One of the board members exclaimed as she pushed her note pad in my direction.

The room filled with laughter as we adjourned the negotiations. My point is: the board has gone through a long hiring process, and they are eager to get you signed. You will never again have the leverage that you have at that moment. Use it to your advantage.

The following is an excerpt from *Friendly Persuasion* by Bob Woolf. I hope it will help you during contract negotiations:

· Try to get the other side to make the first offer.

· Don't get angry because the offer isn't what you wanted.

- Determine how much room they have to move (an offer is an offer—you are negotiating).
- Try to assess their weaknesses. They need you more than you need them.
- Assess your leverage. How was the pool of candidates—do you have the qualifications? Is this your first superintendency?
- Make your presentation logical.
- Start high but don't be ridiculous.
- Have a feel for range of the salary of the job, considering the cost of living.
- Don't give information, get it.
- Make sure the other side knows you want but do not need the job. Do not appear to be begging.
- Be flexible—some people have lost the job in negotiation. Try to make up a loss in another area.
- Keep a record of each conversation. In fact, review the notes before leaving.
- Never raise or lower a figure before you've been asked to do so.
- In your quest for a contract, you have the urge to lower a figure—do not do it until you are asked to by the other side. Do not give tit-for-tat.
- Do not split the difference.
- Don't let them intimidate you: again—they wouldn't be negotiating with you if they weren't interested.
- If you have what you want, don't let it go further. Don't be greedy.
- Don't be afraid to leave something on the table.
- Use common sense.

Principal and Vice Principal Contracts

The superintendent usually negotiates contracts for principals and vice principals. In many cases, especially in larger districts, a salary schedule is already established based on years of experience and educational level. Benefits are usually uniform for all administrators throughout the district.

If you are offered a contract by the school board after an interview, you may want to discuss the contract with them. They may tell you the superintendent will discuss the contract with you.

There is no harm in asking the superintendent if part of the contract is negotiable. You may have a rare situation. Remember a superintendent *is usually a trained negotiator.*

Important Points

1. Prepare your staff for a site visit from a committee.
2. Have a trusted administrator with you in case the committee does not want you as an escort during the site visit.
3. The site visiting committee will observe the appearance of your district, and how you interact with staff, kids, and community members.
4. Do your homework before you go to your first contract negotiation meeting.
5. Make a list of all the items you should consider in your contract.
6. Use your state professional association contract advisor.
7. Be realistic in your contract negotiations.
8. Remember this is the best contract you will get during your tenure in this district. Make it a good one.
9. Principal and vice principal contracts are usually negotiated with the superintendent of schools.

In our sample, Dr. Bright closed the deal. She completed her negotiations, signed her contract, and looked forward with anticipation to her future with the Cripple Creek School District.

Chapter Ten

The Aftermath

Back in your old district

Once the job is won, there is still a great deal of work to be done. A reminder here is that you are already planning for your *next* job. That's right, the one after the contract you just signed. When you get ready to leave the next job, future-hiring districts will contact your current employees and co-workers again.

The first step is to notify your immediate superior of your impending resignation—in person if possible. If not, telephone her—but don't leave a message. Media persons acquire information, and it is transmitted instantaneously. You do not want your bosses to hear of your hire though the media.

Schedule a quick meeting with your office staff and tell them about your new job. Assure them you will be there to support them while hiring your replacement and if they need your help in the future.

If you are a building principal or superintendent, send a message via E-mail to all of your employees with the same information and assurances. Follow it up with a letter because some of your employees may not have access to E-mail.

Within a week, call and thank your character references for their help getting your new job. If you cannot reach them by telephone, send them a handwritten thank you note. Do not forget to call the search consultant and thank her for her help.

You will probably still be under contract for some time before you begin your new job. You will receive telephone calls from your new school district giving you information or asking for decisions. If you are still being paid by your school district, you owe it to them to give them 100%—even if your heart is at your new job.

Inform the new district personnel that you are still under contract and would prefer business calls in the evening or on the weekend. I would also recommend making arrangements with the new district to be able to place collect telephone calls. It would not be proper to have toll calls to your new district appear on your old district's telephone bill.

If you need time off to attend a meeting or help with a new hire at your new district, be sure to use vacation days. Take the opportunity to thank your subordinates and co-workers and say good bye to them.

What if you didn't get the job?

The job search is a very stressful process. What if you don't get the job? Are you a failure? The answers are: it is not the end of the world, and no, you are not a failure.

Reasons for not being selected

No matter how hard you work to cut yourself out from the pack, there are other dynamics over which you have no control.

· There may be an inside candidate and the school district went through the proper steps before hiring her.

· There may be a situation in the district where they need a person of a different color or sex at that particular time.

· Some other candidate may have had an inside track.

· The fit was not just right between the school district and you.

· The winning candidate had experience in an area the district needed, and you did not have the requisite background.

· A better qualified and better prepared candidate won. It happens.

Learn from the experience

Try to find out why you were not selected.

· Check the winner's credentials against yours.

· Call someone on the interview committee and ask her what you can do to improve your interview techniques.

· Call colleagues who may know someone in the district and have them find out

why you were not selected. The hiring district may have talked to a teacher that you had a conflict with. She may have provided them with derogatory information. If so, you can do some damage control before applying for other positions.
· If you didn't get an interview, call the human resources person or search consultant and ask if there was something wrong with your paperwork.

Now what?

Learn from the experience and improve yourself in areas where weaknesses appeared. The job search is a highly stressful process. You will have very high points and low points in your life. In addition, you are probably doing your regular job, so you have extended yourself. Take steps to lower your stress level.

· Practice relaxing.
· Maintain a positive attitude. If you were not a competent person, you would not have your current job.
· Get plenty of rest.
· Eat healthy meals and don't overeat.
· Get plenty of sleep.
· Get plenty of exercise.
· Try not to add any more stress to your life.

Even though you didn't get the position, your ideal job may still be out there. Take the steps now to improve your chances for your next application—and good luck.

Appendix A

Sample interview questions

- How do you see this position fitting into your career goals?
- We are interested in creative solutions to problems and in innovative programs without losing sight of the basics. How do you view yourself as a person who can help us move ahead but not lose the best of what we already have?
- Describe your problem solving skills and give us an example of how you have already used them or might use them on this job.
- Please describe your management or leadership style.
- How do you persuade people to see your point of view and agree to it?
- If we checked two or three of your references, what words would they use to describe you as a leader and a person?
- What are three or four personal qualities that best describe you?
- How would you describe your success at inspiring loyalty, in getting people to want to do the work assigned them, and in developing teamwork?
- What do you consider to be the most important two or three duties of this position?
- How would you operate so that the school board, staff, and community would know you hold yourself accountable for the position that you hold?
- Just where does the buck stop in educational administration?
- Describe a good administrator.
- In as few words as possible, and preferably with an example from your experience, please tell us what your philosophy of education is.
- Define "management team" as you would want it operating in this school or district if you were hired for this position.
- How would you formulate policies in each of these areas: Budgeting? Personnel?
- Public relations? Curriculum? Discipline? Facilities?
- How would you propose to develop long range plans?
- What are the real values of intramural and interscholastic activities to students and the community?
- What experience have you had with goal setting for a school or school district?
- Discipline is a hot topic these days. How would you go about reviewing our written policy?

· Student and staff safety is another hot topic these days. What action would you take to assure student and staff safety?

· With all the push to provide a strong basic education and improved test scores, how would you assure both?

· With the present decreasing in funding for general, special, at-risk, and gifted education programs, how would you insure quality programs are maintained?

· If you had an opportunity to invite a famous person or group to the district for in-service, whom would you invite?

· If you were asked to give a talk about requiring a qualifying high school graduation test, what would you say?

· What is your philosophy for developing the budget? How do you create a budget? Whom do you involve?

· If you were required to reduce a budget after it had been accepted and approved by the school board, what steps would you take?

· If it became a financial reality that either the extracurricular program or the transportation program would have to be eliminated or reduced, how would you decide what to recommend to the school board?

· If you were invited to give a talk to the local community civic leaders with a specific request that you talk about vouchers and charter schools, what would you tell them?

· Suppose that shortly after you moved into this position you were deluged with complaints about an assembly on lesbians and homosexuals. How would you respond to the complaints?

· What are some advantages and disadvantages to having citizens' advisory councils?

· What should your role and the role of the school board be in developing community support for education?

· How do you view the development of administrator's bargaining units below the superintendent level?

· As the negotiator or member of the negotiation team, what do you perceive as a reasonable way to negotiate for the school board without giving everything to the staff?

· If it appears that a teacher strike is imminent, what actions would you recommend to the board? If the strike actually occurred, would you recommend closing the schools or keeping them open with substitutes?

· After the strike, what actions would you pursue to help the healing process?

· As a central office person, how would you communicate with staff members in the buildings?

- What experiences have you had relating to ethnic minorities?
- If you were hired and discovered that the building or district had a morale problem, what action would you take?
- Describe what experiences you have had in sexual harassment cases? Staff? Students?
- What is you philosophy on school safety?
- What do you consider to be your responsibilities in hiring personnel who would report directly to you?
- As a superintendent, what do you feel is the best way for the school board to be involved in hiring teachers and administrators?
- Describe the personal qualities you would seek in people whom you would hire to work with you.
- How do you give people recognition for a job well done?
- If an administrator was not effective, what steps would you take to either improve her effectiveness or release her?
- What consistent actions would you take to insure that your supervisor is kept informed about issues and problems relating to work in the building or district?
- If you were hired for this position, what would you expect from the superintendent or school board in the way of direction and support?
- If the superintendent or school board did not accept your recommendation on a problem or project, how would you deal with the decision?
- You are directed by your supervisor to do something you know to be illegal. What would you do?
- What do you think is a reasonable evaluation process for you if you were hired for this position?
- Please describe to us your method of developing board agenda and preparing the school board to discuss that agenda and vote intelligently?
- How would you work with new board members to help them develop into effective members as quickly as possible?
- A new school board member is elected on the platform of school change. She is disagreeable at board meetings, votes against most items on the agenda, and takes her complaints to the press. What will you do?
- What are the most significant trends in education today?
- If you were doing this interview, what additional question would you like to ask each candidate?
- It seems impossible to be a leader without coming into conflict with someone sooner or later. Please tell us about some conflict you have been involved in and how it was resolved.

· We seek a "whole person" for this position. Briefly tell us about how you use your time off.

A Few Generic Questions

· Who has had the greatest influence on your career?
· What was the most useful criticism you have received?
· Describe the project that best describes your analytical skills.
· What are your team-player qualities?
· What idea have you developed that was particularly creative or innovative?
· What frustrates you the most?
· Give an idea of a situation in which you failed and how you handled it.
· Describe a situation where you had to work with someone who was difficult. · How did you handle the situation?

Appendix B

Sample superintendent contract

Cripple Creek School District
Employment Contract
Superintendent of Schools

It is hereby agreed by and between the Board of Directors ("Board") and [name] ("Superintendent") that the Board, in accordance with its action at a meeting held on [date], has and does hereby employ [name] as Superintendent of the District on the following terms and conditions:

Agreements

1. **Term.** The term of this employment contract is for three years, commencing [date] and ending [date].

2. Professional Responsibilities

   2.1 The Superintendent shall devote his full time and attention to performing faithfully the duties of the Superintendent and Secretary of the Board pursuant to state law and the policies, rules and regulations made thereunder by the board.

   2.2 Subject to Board approval, and any restrictions imposed by law, the Superintendent may organize, reorganize, and arrange the administrative and supervisory staff of the District in the manner that in her judgment best serves the interests of the District. The responsibility for the selection, placement, and transfer of personnel shall be vested in the Superintendent, subject to approval by the Board.

   2.3 The Superintendent, with Board approval, may attend

appropriate professional meetings at the local, state, and national level, the reasonable expenses of which will be borne by the District.

2.4 The Superintendent, with Board approval, may undertake consultive work, speaking engagements, writing, lecturing, or professional duties and obligations which do not conflict with her duties as Superintendent.

2.5 The Superintendent, with Board approval, is authorized to take nine (9) semester hours of advanced degree work per year, the reasonable expenses of which will be borne by the District.

3. **Compensation and Benefits.** For the first year of this employment contract [dates], the Superintendent will receive the following salary and benefits:

3.1 An annual salary of [amount in dollars], payable in equal monthly installments.

3.2 A cost of living increase of 4% of salary the second year and 4% increase of salary the third year of the contract.

3.3 The Superintendent will be included in the District long term disability, life insurance, dental and health insurance programs provided other certificated administrators, and premiums to be paid by the District at the same rate as the other certificated administrators.

3.4 Holidays recognized by the District.

3.5 Twenty-five (25) vacation days annually of legal holidays. Unused vacation days may be carried over to an ensuing year under this contract, up to a total of forty-five (45) days. Such accumulated vacation may be taken in the ensuing year. Unused vacation will be compensated upon termination of employment as Superintendent at the then-applicable salary rate to the extent consistent with law and without causing the district financial penalty. For purposes of computation of per diem rate the superintendent's contract shall be considered to be 223 days.

3.6 Three (3) personal leave days per year.

3.7 Twelve (12) days annual leave with compensation for illness, injury, and emergencies with unused leave to accumulate from year to year to the extent allowed by law. Accrued and unused sick leave may be cashed out pursuant to state and federal laws.

3.8 The costs of membership in the American Association of School Administrators, the State association of school administrators, and other professional groups specifically approved by the Board.

3.9 Membership fees, and costs of meals for the Superintendent's membership in local civic organizations as approved by the Board will be borne by the District.

3.10 The Board shall provide the Superintendent with transportation required in the performance of her official duties. In lieu of other expense reimbursement for in-district travel, the Superintendent shall receive [dollar amount] per month to defray costs incurred in using her automobile for official travel. The Superintendent shall be entitled to out-of-district mileage outside a twenty mile radius of the district, and other expense reimbursement for official business as provided by law and district policy for administrators.

4. Evaluation

4.1 The Board and Superintendent shall meet before the beginning of each school year to establish District goals and objectives for the ensuing school year. These goals and objectives shall be reduced to writing and, to the extent applicable, shall be considered by the Board in evaluating the Superintendent.

4.2 The Superintendent's job performance will be evaluated, prior to June 1, annually by the Board with the results of each evaluation to be made known to the Superintendent.

5. **Termination.** During the term of this employment contract, the Superintendent will be subject to discharge for sufficient cause as provided by law.

6. Miscellaneous.

6.1 The Board of Directors individually and collectively will refer promptly to the Superintendent for study and recommendation all criticism, complaints and suggestions relating to the affairs of the District which are called to its attention.

6.2 The Superintendent agrees to have a comprehensive medical examination and eye examination once each year. A statement certifying to the physical competency of the Superintendent shall be filed with the president of the Board and treated as confidential information by the Board. The cost of such medical report shall be paid by the District.

7. **Contract Review**

7.1 This employment contract shall be reviewed prior to each anniversary date to consider adjustments in compensation and benefits for the ensuing contract year. In connection with each review, the Board and the Superintendent will attempt to agree upon the salary and benefits; absent mutual agreement, the Board will determine the salary and benefits which will not be less than those provided in the current contract year. Any increase in compensation and benefits made during the life of this contract shall be in the form of an amendment, which shall become a part of this contract.

7.2 The contract of the Superintendent will be reviewed by the Board annually on or before June 30 to consider whether or not a new three (3) year contract should be awarded, or whether the on going contract, for expressed reasons, should continue towards its maturity.

8. **Complete Agreement.** This employment contract represents the complete agreement between the parties regarding the employment of the Superintendent by the Board and there are no oral or other written agreements, which modify its terms.

Dated: _____   _____
Superintendent

Dated: _____   _____

President, Board of Directors
Cripple Creek School District

Index

General Resources

Allen, Jeffrey G., J.D., C.P.C. *Jeff Allen's Best: The Résumé*. John Wiley & Sons, 1990.

Allen, Jeffrey G., J.D., C.P.C. *The Perfect Job Reference*, 1990.

Baldridge, Letitia. *The Amy Vanderbilt Complete Book of Etiquette*. Doubleday & Co, 1978.

Bellows, Roger M., *Employment Psychology: The Interview*. Rinehart & Co.1954.

Benson, Herbert, M.D., with Miriam Z. Klipper. *The Relaxation Response*. Avon Books, 1976.

Carnegie, Dale, *How to Win Friends & Influence People*. Simon & Schuster, 1936.

Cavett, Robert. *Success With People Through Human Engineering and Motivation*. Success Unlimited, 1969.

Cohen, Herb. *You Can Negotiate anything*. Bantam Books, 1980.

Fast, Julius. *Body Language*. Pocket books, 1982.

Forem, Jack. *Transcendental Meditation*. E.P. Dutton, 1973.

Ivey, Paul W. *Successful Salesmanship*. 6th edition.Prentice-Hall, 1942.

Lopez, Felix M., Jr. *Personnel Interviewing Theory and Practice*. McGraw-Hill Book Company, 1965.

Maltz, Maxwell. *Psycho-Cybernetics*. Pocket Books, 1966.

Martin, Judith. *Miss Manners' Guide to Excruciatingly correct Behavior*. Atheneum, 1982.

Molloy, John T. *Dress for Success*. Warner Books, 1978.

Molloy, John T. *The Woman's Dress For Success Book*. Warner Books, 1978.

Noble, David F, Ph.D. *Professional Résumés for Executives, Managers, and Other Administrators*. JIST Works, Inc., 1998.

Peale, Norman Vincent. *The Power of Positive thinking.* Prentice-Hall, 1952.

Ringer, Robert J. *Looking Out for Number One.* Fawcett Crest Books, 1978.

Tarrant, John. *Perks and Parachutes.* Simon & Schuster, 1985.

Waitley, Denis E.,Ph.D. *The Psychology of Winning.* Nightingale-Conant, 1979.

Walters, Barbara. *How to Talk With Practically Anybody about Practically Everything.* Doubleday, 1970.

Warschaw, Tessa Albert. *Winning Through Negotiations.* McGraw Hill, 1980.

Zunin, Leonard, with Zunin, Natalie. *Contact-The first four Minutes.* Nash Publishing Company, 1972.

Order Information

Tear out this sheet and give it to a friend so that he/she may order a book:

Telephone Orders:

To order, please contact customer service at 1-877-823-9235, Monday through Friday, 9:00 AM to 6:00 PM, Central Standard Time

On Line order:

Visit our web site at www.iuniverse.com, 24 hours a day, seven days a week, to order on line Or generate a printable order form that can be faxed to 1-402-323-7824.

Please note that we accept Visa, Mastercard, American Express, and cashier's checks or money orders.

Printed in the United States
44383LVS00003B/297

9 780595 091492